New World Meditation

NEW
WORLD
MEDITATION

Focusing-Mindfulness-Healing-Awakening

Lucinda Gray Ph.D.
with
David William Truslow

NEW WORLD MEDITATION

Focusing-Mindfulness-Healing-Awakening

By

Lucinda Gray Ph.D.

with

David William Truslow

NEW BUDDHA
B O O K S
LA   CA   USA

NEW WORLD MEDITATION
A New Buddha Book
Los Angeles, California

Contents

Introduction

Lucinda Gray PhD

The experience of daily practice in New World Meditation (NWM) is similar in form to a spiral. It begins at the surface of the mind with the superficial happenings of the day and gradually turns inward, deepening into the self. The challenge of this book was to put this essentially nonlinear form into chapters and order them in a sequence that made sense to us. The structure we came to evolved gradually over many months as David and I struggled with the complexity of the material.

With this spiral form we return again and again to basic concepts. Dropping judgment is one of these essential elements. At first it may simply seem like an interesting idea, but as your practice deepens into more advanced stages you will see how important and profoundly difficult it is. This book is very condensed. Each chapter is like a window into the evolution of daily practice: learning how to meditate, building a regular practice, learning how to deal with the interruptions and the graspings, deepening into core issues, resolving them in a process of emotional healing, and continuing to move deeper. Ultimately you come to Awakening, the flowering of your essential self into your full potential.

This book is as much about healing as it is about learning to meditate. The healing we describe here is generic in nature. In using the word generic I am saying that the stages of the healing process are always the same no matter the method. It is always a process of re-owning your true self. The big advantage of NWM is the daily practice that softly and naturally but relentlessly continues to move you along the healing path. It is so gentle and gradual that the power of the process only reveals itself over months and years.

We will show you how to reconnect to your true self, buried under all the defenses you have created during your lifetime. Gradually you forge a constant strong connection to your core sense of self, the wisdom you carry deep in your body. You are always in touch with your values; you know what is important to you, what you need and don't need, and understand why. This changes your perspective on yourself and your life as a whole, freeing up your energy for health, happiness, human connection and creative pursuits.

Most of us live our lives in stress and unhappiness. We are not even aware of the pain because this is our only reality. It's like the wallpaper, always there, and so it goes unnoticed. We are constantly trying to meet the expectations of our parents and what we perceive as the requirements of society, rather than following our own personal truth. This inner conflict between our true self and our compliant, conforming personality causes severe emotional and physiological stress, making us unhappy and increasing our vulnerability to disease.

This abandonment of our true nature is rooted in fear of our feelings. Our feelings are inconvenient. They aren't always in tune with parental or societal expectations, so we learn very early to push them out of awareness. We proceed to do what is expected of us at home, at school and later at work and in relationships. Our self-abandonment is so complete that we lose all connection to our true feelings, which dwell in the body, and adopt the "pseudo feelings" we think are expected. I call them "pseudo feelings" because they have no connection to body experience, so they are not really feelings at all.

The good news is that wallpaper can be changed. The healing we are describing means giving up the defense of grandiosity, letting go of pretending that you are immune from hurt, and acknowledging your vulnerability. Ironically, this is immensely strengthening because it is the truth, rather than a false pretense. Yes, you are human, you have feelings, and they are an asset not a liability. They guide you toward doing what feels good rather than what you think is expected.

Being a therapist myself and having received great therapy, I trust the process of psychotherapy to heal the wounds of life. Yet I have come to believe that this daily practice may be more effective than therapy in improving physical and mental health and healing the injuries of the past. Even after therapy life goes on, always confronting us with new challenges that must be overcome. NWM is always there for you to rely on, a lifetime path of personal enrichment and a source of inner peace.

There is something transformational about spending quiet time with yourself, even for fifteen minutes each day. This is why we say that healing starts as soon as you begin your practice. Repeating the act of meditating daily reinforces a certain loyalty-to-self that says I love myself, I will take care of myself and I will heal myself. This loyalty-to-self strengthens each time you sit, at the same time that it reinforces your connection to your core self.

Some of what you find out about yourself – your past injuries, your anger, rage and your neediness – will not be easy. But you will also discover wonderful things: your creativity, your joy, and your ability to give and to receive love. We all have injuries. Acknowledging emotionally painful events is something we avoid as long as possible. The more serious the trauma, the more upsetting it is to discover the truth and admit all of it to yourself. Then in order to feel whole and complete, you must come to self-empathy, self-forgiveness and compassion. Yes, healing takes time, but relief is amazing, so liberating and so profound that it changes your life.

It was this way for me. As I healed I was different, and I didn't want to go back. I felt as if I couldn't go back; the old way simply didn't work for me anymore. Now I understand why going back is impossible. Healing actually changes your core operating system. The parameters by which you understand the world and guide your life are not the same anymore, so there really is no way to retreat.

Awakening is the culmination of healing. You are more authentic and immensely more loyal to your true nature. Your body is fully alive, no longer numbed out and ignored. Your feelings are now a vast resource of information constantly available to you. The Body/Mind Wisdom, this merging of mind knowing with body knowing, is an entirely new and vastly expanded level of consciousness. Now you are free to be fully yourself and live your full potential. Your new world is always forward, toward expanding awareness and self-realization.

L.G. 6-5-14

David William Truslow

There are only three things you can do to increase the ability of the brain to adapt: computer games designed for that purpose, exercise, and meditation. The effects of meditation are so powerful that even the military wants to use mindfulness to make super-warriors that are smarter and capable of calm and sustained concentration in battle. Meditation actually changes the brain structure making some areas thicker, including the prefrontal cortex (research funded by the DOD), and some thinner. Also, meditation reduces stress, and stress is a cause or contributor to 90% of all illness and disease. So starting and continuing a meditation practice seems a logical choice for anyone who wants to maintain and improve physical and mental health.

All of us can benefit from meditation, but unfortunately it is difficult to begin and establish a daily practice. Part of this difficulty is not having the tools from Focusing that you will learn to use in New World Meditation. I did have a practice of mindfulness growing up, which I couldn't put a label on, so it seemed a natural part of my life. I spent hours by myself, manipulating toys when I was younger and then fixing things around the house as I got older. I found working with my hands very soothing. As a teenager I often went overnight camping alone in the nearby mountains. I loved the sky, the shapes of clouds, the shadows coming and going, the stars moving across the night. By holding very still I let the animals come out so that I could observe them. I reassured myself that even without the conveniences, my life is sustainable and naturally beautiful. Partly as a result of these wonderful times, I formed a negative attitude toward conventional values. I knew that even if I couldn't grow up to be a rocket scientist, I would be happy as a carpenter. I didn't really enjoy academic life until I was in college.

In my seventh grade English class we were given an assignment to write about our favorite pet peeve. As the class read their essays, I was struck by how different we are from those around us and began to wonder where these marked differences came from. How is our personal reality formed? I didn't really have the concept of personal reality, but I had heard the expression "what makes us tick." I already knew from being an only child with seven brothers and sisters that my two sets of parents each had their own agenda, quite separate from my own. I was now pondering how they came to believe what they thought was good for me.

Over the years I had strong emotional reactions to some events and wondered where they came from. I struggled to figure it out. I tried to remember the last time I had this same feeling, and then went back in time, searching for the earliest incident that felt the same. Often these feelings went back to my childhood. Of course, this rarely worked; there were lots of dead ends and time lags between when I first had the feeling and when I wondered where it came from. I was also dependent on my memory, which I now realize is often blocked by defenses.

When I was introduced to Focusing I discovered that I could use my body's knowing to find the source of my feelings. What a relief. Now I had a method, I didn't have to rely on memory alone. I could use my felt sense of events to understand their meaning. This is the tool I was missing in my quest to understand what made me "tick." With Focusing I was no longer stuck in old patterns I could work through my childhood baggage and come to a feeling of resolution.

Lucinda wanted me to meditate because my business was so taxing, not to mention our high speed life style in Los Angeles. I knew I needed stress reduction, but in the past when I did try to meditate I could never relax, I had so many interruptions. Thirteen years ago we started meditating together. After each sitting Lucinda asked me how it went. At first there was so much going on that she taught me to use clearing a space (from Focusing) to set aside the chatter, such as: call the accountant, stop by the cleaners, fix the garage door, and so on. With clearing a space as a tool, my mind got a lot quieter and I began to benefit from the stress reduction. Of course there were still interruptions, but now they were more meaningful; they were things I needed to resolve. Then, between clearing out, resolving and setting aside, I was sometimes able to get to a clear space; a most wonderful state of relaxation, even when it only lasted for a few moments.

As the months passed I still had interruptions that I could not resolve, but now I had inner quiet and concentration to work on them. It turns out those pesky interruptions are the key to insight. Not only was I discovering what formed the basis of my needs, wants and desires, I was now changing the parameters I used to make decisions. Old injuries and fears were no longer controlling my world view. Getting to the truth of what happened was difficult, but the rewards of self-forgiveness were so powerful I was fully motivated to keep up my daily practice.

New World Meditation, this hybrid of mindfulness and Focusing, moves fast. I gained insight much more quickly than when I was just Focusing alone. I was able to process and heal most of my painful memories, but even after I came to peace with all this, I still have a core of self-blame that keeps coming up. Before healing I spent a lot of time and energy beating up on myself. Now I pull out of it more rapidly. I recognize that some of the key events that shaped my personal reality happened before I had memory or language. That is why these things are so difficult to resolve. I have a body sense of these early events, but it is hard to find words and/or images that fit, and then come to a felt shift, and full relief. The only thing that helps is self-empathy, connecting with the infant and small child I once was, and reminding myself that this feeling I carry inside is what I must have felt as a baby or toddler. From this place I can get to self-compassion, feeling for and with my little self, so dependent and so vulnerable. Self-compassion changes everything.

It changes my outlook on these early assumptions: I'm a bad boy, it must be my fault. I can finally release self-blame, at least sometimes I can. I'm on my way. This is my Awakening.

Our defenses protect us from pain, but they also prevent us from accessing our emotional and intuitive knowing. Healing removes these defenses, which opens the body's wisdom to cognitive thought. In this book we call it the Body/Mind Wisdom. I like to think of this blessing as "fully conscious living," and I have every confidence you can enjoy it too.

D.W.T. 6-10-14

NEW
WORLD
MEDITATION

NEW BUDDHA BOOKS

PART ONE:
INTRODUCING NEW WORLD
MEDITATION

One

The Makeup of Personal Reality

The purpose of Mindfulness practice (Vipassana), in the Buddhist view, is to see things as they really are. We believe that to see things as they really are requires that we first and most importantly see ourselves as we really are. After all, it is through our own senses and mind that we take in and make meaning from all that we experience.

Current research in neuroscience is exploding with so many new discoveries about the structure and workings of the human brain that scientists can hardly keep up with it. Here you will find a very condensed version of what neuroscientists and psychologists now believe about how we build our personal reality. It is organized in such a way as to help you to understand how you came to see the world and yourself as you do, so that you can more easily comprehend the healing journey of New World Meditation.

The brain is an extremely complex processing system, in which connections are made via chemical/electrical transmissions. All incoming data are filtered and analyzed through our unique perceptual and interpretive equipment, the brain and mind. Here we are using the word "brain" to the organ contained in the skull and connected to every cell in the body through the nervous and endocrine systems. The mind is the set of parameters that we each develop through experience and learning as we grow. In metaphoric terms we think of the brain as the hardware and the mind as the operating system.

The brain works automatically to route incoming data to specific areas for processing. The mind/operating system develops through learning. For example, the brain discriminates between different frequencies of visible light. It is the mind/operating system that through learning, labels these frequencies as different colors – red, blue, yellow – and decides that we stop at a red light.

The mind and brain function as one, fully enmeshed and interconnected. They grow together organically, each affecting the development and ultimate shape of the other, in a continuous process of expansion, elaboration, modification and further expansion. Our nerve endings are connected to the various senses, specific functions of the brain, constantly taking in information from which the mind creates meaning. They also connect to the motor functions through which we act upon the world. The brain and mind are continuously adapting as we integrate newly acquired information.

The deepest part of the brain, which includes the brain stem, was earliest to evolve. It is called the hindbrain, or reptilian brain. It works automatically on primary functions such as maintaining your breathing, your heartbeat and your digestion. Overlaid on the hindbrain is the midbrain, or mammalian brain, which evolved much later. This is the area of the brain where emotions and basic drives originate. It is the source of emotional responses and the place where affect-loaded memories are stored.

In evolutionary terms the most recently developed part of the brain is the cerebral cortex, particularly the prefrontal region. It is the functioning of the prefrontal cortex that distinguishes us from apes and other advanced mammals. This is the part of the brain where we have the capacity for problem-solving and abstract reasoning. In addition, it holds our potential for advanced levels of consciousness such as self-reflection, empathy, generosity, gratitude, and eventually self-forgiveness and compassion.

The mind is a complex set of underlying attitudes, assumptions and parameters through which we interpret all the input from the senses and then choose our behavioral responses. The development of the mind begins with the very earliest experiences. Each layer of experience that makes up the operating system is overlaid upon and modified by the ones before. Thus we gradually construct this very elaborate set of parameters.

Our personal reality is shaped by the massive amount of information we take in as we grow and develop, and the meaning we make from that information. From the moment of conception we are constantly learning about ourselves and the world around us. Babies begin to learn in the womb. Through hearing we become accustomed to the tones of language and learn to recognize mother's voice as distinct from others. At the sound of her voice, we develop a sense of comfort, which is one of the earliest components of the operating system. (Stern, 2012)

In infancy and early childhood we direct all our energy toward discovering what is going on around us and what it means. Babies are always hungrily taking in and integrating information. They are learning to recognize events and their consequences so that they can predict what will happen next. There is tremendous urgency in baby's concentrated attention to the world around her. This drive for understanding is a basic survival mechanism, a continuous process of pattern recognition. The speed and accuracy of pattern recognition is referred to as fluidity and measured by IQ tests, the most generally accepted of which are the Wechsler Intelligence Scales. (Wechsler, 1958)

The meaning we take from all this input gradually forms the basic components of the mind, which is constantly increasing in complexity. The earliest components of the mind take the form of "If this then that; if this happens then that will follow." We learn very early in life that hot causes pain, and mommy's smile means food/love. Every experience initiates a specific and unique sequence of synaptic firings in the brain. When these sequences are repeated again and again, patterns are established that eventually become stable and resistant to change. These patterns are primary components of the mind.

Our capacity to take in information and the speed with which we process it accelerates rapidly, especially as we acquire language. We assign meaning and relative importance to every piece of information. Any emotionally powerful experience, whether negative or positive, will naturally carry greater importance in forming the parameters through which we interpret what is going on and choose our responses.

The mind is under construction all during childhood and adolescence, when the brain is growing rapidly. The brain continues to grow until we reach the age of about 24. There are major physiological changes, important developmental milestones, at age 7, 13, and again at 18. At these critical periods the brain reaches new levels of maturity, making more advanced reasoning possible. This process is continuous until the brain is fully developed. At that time the mind is well-established and works automatically. For the most part it operates outside our awareness, always filtering and interpreting our sensory input.

The earliest sense of identity is formed in this same way. As the baby crawls around the floor she builds an image of herself, a primitive identity based on the discovery of her body boundary, a sense of where she ends and the outside world begins. This is a kinesthetic process of self-discovery through touch and body sensation. (Gray, 1977)

The most important patterns that form the operating system come from the quality of the bonds we form with parents in the first two years of life. (Stern, 2012) Our unique, custom-designed view of the world evolves from what we learn in these primary relationships. All through life our responses to the world and to people depend upon what happened in those earliest days. Yet we have no conscious memories of this primary experience because it comes before we have language.

The earlier in life an experience takes place the more impact it will have on long-term development of the mind. The earliest experiences hold great power because infants have no basis for comparison, no framework through which to evaluate the relative importance of any particular event. Each moment of life looms large in the world of the infant, in her constant effort to understand and assign meaning. We imagine that the world of the infant is like sitting in the front row of a movie theatre with huge images floating above.

Neuroscience research over the past 30 years has shown that the personality of the child is shaped in the first two months of life, in the bonding relationship with the mother or caretaker. This earliest relationship creates lasting response patterns; children have the same basic personality structure at age 6 as they have at two months of age. (Stern, 2000)

Our definition of love is established in the first months of life, based on the experience of mother's care. Her smile is associated with food and affection, the comfort of being held, and the consistent message of unconditional love that she conveys with her gaze and her touch. Based on all this input we build an embedded pattern of synaptic firings that we interpret as love. This pattern lasts throughout life and can only be modified through a deep and profound process of self-reflection. (Lewis, Amini, Lannon, 2001)

Negative experiences in this early bonding process also feed into the operating system. Babies learn quickly that some things lead to negative outcomes. When mommy is angry, her voice turns harsh and she withdraws her loving attention. Baby learns to behave in such a way as to avoid this painful experience.

It is thought, though not yet proven, that preverbal memories are stored in the midbrain, in the form of images, smells and sounds. They are not readily available to ordinary consciousness. This midbrain memory holds many of the neural patterns that determine our responses to the events of life. All through life we will be drawn to the tones of voice and smells that are similar to those we experience at the breast. They have a powerful influence over our choice of a mate, yet because these patterns are established before we have language they operate unconsciously and automatically.

Negative events, traumatic memories, are powerful learning experiences that are never forgotten. It is essential to our survival that we avoid a repetition. Therefore every detail is retained in memory. It is believed that these threatening memories are also stored in the midbrain – in the amygdala, part of the limbic system. Normally we go along in life until something happens that reminds us of the original painful event. Then we experience a strong disproportionate emotional reaction, which we do not understand.

Learning continues all through life. It seems logical that the mind is modified as we take in sensory data. What I find more amazing is the new discovery that the mind influences the physiological development of the brain itself. Activities we engage in and feelings we experience not only shape the development of the mind, they alter patterns of synaptic firing in the brain and ultimately change even the physiology of the brain itself. Scientists refer to this as the neuroplasticity of the brain. This has been confirmed through research with PET scans. (Lazar et al., 2005) This quality of brain plasticity gives us an amazing ability to adapt to new learning. Even long-established patterns of synaptic firing can be changed through new experience (Siegel, 2007) Recent research confirms that meditation, specifically Mindfulness practice, twenty minutes per day for only eight weeks measurably enlarges the prefrontal cortex. (Lazar et al., 2005)

Experience in the Creation of Meaning

Our reality is not a set of universally accepted truths, as we tend to believe. Rather it is complex, personal and unique to each of us. It can be thought of as a metaphoric onion, but unlike the onion with its discrete layers, the parameters – the rules of the system – are not clearly separate. They cannot be understood easily because they are fully integrated into a seamless whole. Each layer grows organically from the raw material of new experience, taken in and synthesized within the pre-existing mind, which is then modified to accommodate the new learning, and so on, in the continuous flow of ongoing experience.

To complicate matters further, it is not easy to fully comprehend the uniqueness of each of us. To begin with, we come into the world with different DNA, and are born into different families. Each parent has his/her own operating system, which they pass on to us through their words, their beliefs and attitudes, and how they relate to us. Their reality is the product of their own experience, their parents and grandparents' experiences and operating systems, going back through thousands of generations.

This is why we feel so alone. We are alone in our uniqueness. What we share is the human condition, our inherent aloneness, and our powerful longing for connection. When it comes to understanding why we make the decisions we do, how we create our blessings or mistakes, whatever form they take, most of us have only very limited awareness. We may have a list of rational mental reasons why we make the choices that shape our path, but there is much more to know, which is hidden deep inside.

This is our situation; the baseline from which we begin our journey of self-discovery. The purpose of our daily practice, like Vipassana, is to see things as they really are. Our task is to bring awareness to the parameters of our operating system, to understand their roots in our experience and how they shape our reality.

New World Meditation is the journey of understanding and healing upon which we embark. Our tools in this endeavor are self-reflection and self-enquiry. Self-reflection is mindfully looking within. Self-enquiry is our way of bringing clarity to our feelings and their meaning. With self-reflection and self-enquiry comes insight, the light of understanding. Insight leads to healing and self-acceptance. As we bring our operating system into full awareness, we see how it came to be as it is, and the defenses we built to ward off pain. Healing frees us from these defenses, and our operating system is changed in the process. Thus healing is the only way we can see ourselves as we really are, and the only path to Awakening.

Two

A New Path

New World Meditation (NWM) is a unique and powerful practice that frees you to live in your true nature. It is a daily ritual of sitting with yourself that eases you gently into a transformational healing process. You are happier, more comfortable and relaxed both physically and mentally. It works by activating your full consciousness, what we call the Body/Mind Wisdom. Now you stream both feeling and thought simultaneously, a far more advanced consciousness than either feeling or thought alone. This enriches every moment of your life.

Our new path is rooted in two sources of knowing: from the Old World, the ancient method of Mindfulness, taught by the Buddha twenty-five hundred years ago, and from the New World, the Focusing method developed by Eugene Gendlin and rooted in the uniquely American Client Centered tradition. This new practice is supported by current knowledge from neuroscience, and the research underlying Focusing, which demonstrate the critical factors that make change, personal growth and healing possible. NWM brings Focusing and Mindfulness together synergistically, to create an experience that is different than either of these.

Because I was a seeker on the path, I was blessed to learn both of these wonderful ways at the same time in my life. I wanted time for both Focusing and meditation, but I only had about thirty minutes to myself each morning, so, I naturally merged them together into one daily practice that was emotionally healing, stress reducing and brought me moments of blissful peace. I practiced this method for years, but it wasn't until I began to teach it to my husband David that I realized I was doing something far different from traditional Mindfulness practice. In order to teach him I had to clearly define my process. This book is the story of our journey as we worked together to elucidate this new healing practice.

I have come to believe that meditation is food for the soul, concentrated food that is very nurturing. It is a special, high-quality form of attention that only you can give, much more fulfilling than just sitting around thinking. It satisfies a deep hunger we all share: the need to connect with self.

When I began my graduate training, I tried meditation for relaxation, stress reduction and concentration. I was fascinated by the idea that it might bring me to a higher level of consciousness, and I was looking forward to a great adventure. It was a time of major transition for me. I was recently divorced, a single mother with two small children. There was far more to do than there were hours in the day. Like so many children of alcoholic parents, I needed to feel a sense of control. Starting early every morning I cleaned the house as fast as I could, running from task to task. I was creating this stress to bind my anxiety. I couldn't tolerate leaving a bed unmade or unwashed dishes in the sink. I would race off to school, driving across town in heavy traffic with my heart racing. One morning I had a flash of insight. I realized that it was more important to put myself together than to put the house together.

This was a turning point for me. I began to make meditation a priority. I gave myself permission to sit in silence, going within, every morning before facing the intensity of the day. From the beginning I felt more relaxed. It reduced my anxiety and gave me a serene refuge, a home base in my busy life.

I began with Transcendental Meditation, and then moved to basic Mindfulness practice, which I continued for a number of years. Later I was introduced to Tibetan Buddhist visualization for attaining a deep meditative state while enhancing the power of concentration. I have continued to study Eastern traditions for many years, both Hindu and Buddhist, and have attended seminars with master teachers. I immersed myself in learning about meditation along with mastering the arts of Focusing and psychotherapy.

Establishing the daily discipline wasn't easy for me and it won't be easy for you. But I believe you too will find the rewards are well worth the commitment. Regular meditation meant I had to get up long before my children, which wasn't easy. But it was very rewarding from the start. I reached moments of ecstatic bliss even in the early months. My practice quickly became a treat to look forward to. There were mornings when I had to choose between eating and meditating and I chose to meditate. I found it to be the most satisfying way to spend the small amount of time reserved for me.

My practice changed my life. The relaxing effects lasted all day. I experienced clarity of mind I never knew before and I was able to stay calm even under stress. My priorities were effortlessly clear. I was able to do one thing at a time, putting my full attention on any particular task. I no longer lived with the tension of constantly feeling behind schedule. I was present in the moment and much happier, even when the dishes didn't get done.

In my graduate program I realized the importance of the body as a source of knowing that cannot be ignored. Body psychotherapy originated with Wilhelm Reich, a student of Freud in the Vienna Psychoanalytic Society. It has blossomed into a wide range of therapeutic methods that attempt to access the ongoing flow of feeling-based knowing and the early preverbal memories that current thinkers believe are stored in the body. After completing my doctorate I undertook a six- year training in Integrative Body Psychotherapy. In this training I came to a deep respect for the wisdom of the body. From my own personal experience in recovering early memories I came to believe that they can be accessed only through connecting directly to the body voice. Feelings are carried in the body; the body is the realm of the unconscious. This truth is central to our practice.

Focusing is a revolutionary, research-based method of healing and change that is now being taught all over the world. It is quite easy to learn and does not require special hands-on techniques such as therapeutic massage or acupressure. Over many years of professional practice and in my own inner work, I learned that Focusing offers a clearly articulated pathway to the vast stream of information carried in the body.

Felt sensing is this direct pathway. We enter the felt sense through sensation and emotion. Felt sensing allows us to hear and understand the body voice. I know that no lasting change can happen without a bodily-felt difference. We have to feel something shift inside; otherwise we are likely to revert to old patterns. I have come to believe that felt sensing is the way this key inner feeling shift happens in all therapeutic practices, even those in which the concept is not known. It is an elemental change process.

Focusing works in so many ways: as an integral part of therapy, as a way of self-healing, in partnership with another

Focuser, for creative process and as a method of conflict resolution. I have been a Focusing teacher for many years, and I was one of the first to become a Coordinator and join the leadership circle of the Focusing Institute. As we continue you will learn more about how we apply the tools of Focusing in this new practice.

In this book David and I offer you our wisdom: all that we learned together, and what we each learned in our personal journey of healing and transformation. Along with this I bring you the fruit of my professional experience working with clients and students who struggle to heal, grow and advance in consciousness.

The Path Ahead

Ours is a continuing path of self-discovery, healing and spiritual growth. You cannot now imagine all the wonders that this practice will bring to your life. It offers you great richness and joy in your daily experience and the promise of inner peace born of self-acceptance, self-forgiveness and self-love. It means having a deep and solid sense of connection to your true feelings and needs, a new inner security and trust. You will guide your life from this higher level of awareness, which takes the worry out of making the right decisions along the way. Self-forgiveness is the healing we offer here. With this healing you have the capacity for deep connection with others, and for a lasting, loving and fully sexual intimate relationship. All this is possible for you, in this lifetime.

This is a journey into unexplored territory. It reminds me of hiking into the mountains with a heavy pack. It is more and more beautiful the higher you climb. All along the way it changes. In the beginning the trail might be steep, and then there are easier stretches when it seems you can breathe more deeply.

Sometimes the path is rugged; there are rocky hairpin switch-backs when progress is halting. You might stumble and fall. But if you just concentrate on that one next step, just today's meditation, you will continue to progress. Each time you sit with yourself is like taking that step. All you need to think about is today's practice. Am I willing to sit down this morning to meet with myself, no matter where it leads?

On my last backpacking trip I went with my two strong grown sons. I was in my 50s and my pack seemed to get heavier as I climbed. When I got winded my sons offered to take a share of my burden and little by little I handed off parts of my load.

As the day wore on I found myself looking greedily ahead toward the next curve. I was sure that the campground was right around that corner just up ahead. But when I reached the bend I saw only another upward stretch of trail and another corner to turn. It seemed to go on forever. On that backpacking trip I kept thinking of the goal; I wasn't able to enjoy the journey one step at a time. Now I know that the journey would have been easier and much more fun if I could have been present in the moment.

Finally we reached the ridge line, where we saw a beautiful view. We stopped there, dropped our packs, drank some water and enjoyed the vista. I was elated by the beauty, and felt a great sense of accomplishment. From that point on I could stay in the moment. Reaching that ridge line didn't mean the struggle was over. Slowly we continued up to a peak we could see ahead. In the distance we saw yet another even higher peak. Reaching it would mean climbing over a cascade of boulders but we were undaunted. When we reached the campground we pitched our tents on the shore of a beautiful lake.

Our new path is like this. Like hiking, it requires willingness, dedication and perseverance. As you go along you will eventually meet up with all your baggage, all the hurt, anger, resentment and misunderstanding of the past. Little by little you will encounter the pain of past injuries and fears of the future, and work them through with the tools we offer here. You will gradually unload the weight, but instead of having someone else carry it, you will simply set it down as you make peace with the past. As you go along you will come to understand, accept and heal these old wounds one at a time and the burden gets lighter.

The journey of Awakening is not without challenge, but it is richly rewarding. Like hiking up the mountain, it builds strength and personal resilience. With healing you gradually let go of old baggage at the same time that you are building confidence that you can handle whatever comes next. Ultimately you will be unencumbered and free to live joyously in the present moment.

Only when you are clear about what you want and need can you make the choices that will guide you toward true happiness. It is through your commitment to self-reflection that you will grow your ability to discern your most central intentions. Here you will learn specific methods that support you in building and sustaining a daily practice. Remember that you only need to meditate today, one day at a time. It may encourage you to know that everything you need to change and grow is easily available, already there inside you, awaiting your attention.

Consciousness Expands Through Self-Reflection

Here we are using the term consciousness to denote the ability to watch the workings of your own mind. It includes the perceptions, thoughts, feelings and needs that form the fabric of your deepest nature. It is an inner sensing of the whole of who you are: body, mind and spirit. This inner connection shapes your view of the world, which in turn guides your decision-making. Thus the limits of your consciousness define your experience of life. We believe that pushing these limits and expanding the boundaries of awareness is the most efficient way to gain insight into your true needs and set your intention on a course of action that will meet those needs.

Our capacity to self-reflect is not new. It evolved gradually over many millennia until we developed consciousness. We now believe this evolution was made possible by the expansion of the cerebral cortex, specifically the frontal lobes of the brain. This area of the brain is very small, and is the most recently evolved.

Meditation is the oldest known method specifically designed to maximize our potential for self-reflection. It originated in India, about 5000 years ago, in the religious practice of yoga and Hinduism. Its purpose was to experience one's connection with the Gods. The Buddha lived much later, in the sixth century B.C.E., and he was disenchanted with traditional religious practices. He used meditation to cultivate the realization of the interconnectedness of all things. Today Mindfulness meditation is used in the West most frequently as a way of understanding the workings of the mind and sustaining mental health, rather than as a religious practice.

Most traditional meditation practices provide something for you to concentrate upon as a basic structure to guide you as you go inward. Three methods are commonly taught: mantra recitation, imagery, and Mindfulness. In developing NWM, we use a simple Mindfulness practice: following and counting your breaths. This is the pattern you will always return to. It is an ancient Hindu practice that was rediscovered by the Buddha, and which he taught as a universal remedy. The Buddha's goal was to see things as they really are, to see the reality of the Four Noble Truths. He believed that practicing Mindfulness over a long period of time would lead to a balanced mind full of love and compassion. This practice is now called Vipassana. It is an observation-based, self-exploratory journey. It is quite popular in the West, where it is sometimes called "Insight Meditation."

Meditation in the West

In the West we have a long tradition of Christian meditation sustained for centuries primarily by monks and nuns, and also as part of the Quaker tradition. However, the practice of meditation is unfamiliar to most of us. We have never tried to sit silently for even a few minutes on a daily basis. We almost never see our parents or teachers meditating. This is in contrast to the experience in Asia where families traditionally sit together. Even small children learn to meditate this way.

Here in the Western World we haven't fully appreciated the power of meditation for self-exploration. There are a number of reasons for this. In Buddhism the goal of Vipassana is to see things as they really are, yet it offers no direct path to this clarity. The long search for this missing ingredient has given birth to all of psychotherapy, the awareness movement, encounter groups, personal growth and self-help practices, and even the research into the benefits of psychedelic drugs.

The popularity of pop psychology in America attests to our hunger for any method of self-reflection that might bring better health, new insight and self-awareness, not to mention our longing for a happier life. Yet we have so little time. Clients and students I work with have a hard time beginning and sustaining a regular practice. Most of them are under tremendous stress because of long working hours and commuting time. They are already getting up at 5:30 AM just to get to the office. In order to meditate in the morning they have to get up even earlier. In the evening they are so tired that they fall asleep when they try to meditate. Regular meditation is the very medicine they need, yet they are caught up in the time-crunch dilemma.

There is also a central conflict between Eastern and Western thinking. In Buddhist thought, clearing the mind and bringing the mind to stillness is the precursor to Nirvana, ecstatic bliss. Misconstruing this idea has led many Westerners to believe that when thoughts or feelings come up in meditation we have failed. We are not doing it "right." And so we become discouraged. This is sadly unrealistic because interruptions are to be expected. They are a normal part of all meditation.

Another problem is that meditation is often taught in America as a way to avoid and bypass feelings. The hope is that we can transcend the body and the uncomfortable feelings it carries. This is a big mistake, because it closes this door to the healing potential of your personal truth. And thus it limits self-reflection. Westerners who learn meditation this way sometimes space out into imagery or fantasy. They may experience a state of bliss in which they let go of all feelings, issues or problems, and even float above the body. This certainly reduces stress, which is beneficial, but it is not a process of self-reflection and so it cannot contribute to lasting change, healing or personal growth.

Using meditation to avoid feelings is actually counterproductive. I know people who believe they have mastered meditation, but continue to suffer the pain of anxiety, unhealed trauma and life situations that are not working for them. For them meditation is a source of comfort, but used this way it functions as a defense, putting up a wall so that they learn to reject and ignore troublesome feelings. They are ignoring their body voice that is calling out to be heard.

Misusing meditation is understandable because of the anxiety and restlessness most people experience when they begin daily practice. It is difficult to tolerate these common experiences without an actual method for working with them, a method of self-enquiry. Because of this difficulty many beginners are tempted to give up. Sadly, giving up is forfeiting the healing potential along with the wonderful benefits of stress reduction.

This is the reason why New World Meditation is so needed. We include the essential tools you need to acknowledge and work through interruptions, including anxiety and restlessness. It is what we do with the interruption that is unique. Many of the interruptions are incidental and transient. You will find that these hold only minor importance. We will teach you how to acknowledge them so that they are easily set aside. You can put them away for now, like the things in my backpack that I was able to hand off along the trail.

More powerful feelings will naturally emerge as you move through minor interruptions. Whatever is still unresolved within you will eventually come up, asking for your attention. These are often childhood memories or feelings about incomplete relationships with people who are important in your life. It is this more powerful material that demands self-enquiry and emotional healing. This is a need we all share, since we all carry difficult, uncomfortable and painful feelings, memories, thoughts and images from the past. Until we work through this material we have trouble living in the present moment and guiding our lives in a direction that makes us happy.

The body has its own powerful built-in force for health. Feelings come up in meditation because they need attention, recognition and healing. These feelings direct you inward, toward the valuable information about your truth that you carry in your body. You will learn to use the tools we teach here to work through and heal whatever emerges.

It is the integration of mind and body knowing that makes this such a powerful way of emotional healing. Through your practice you will learn how to listen to and make sense of your body voice, which will contribute to your physical as well as emotional health. Emotional healing is a transformational process leading to resolution and relief from long-term pain and dysfunction. It is emotional healing that puts you on the path to Awakening.

Focusing

We all have what we think of as intuition. We have many ways of talking about this. We might say, "I had a gut feeling about him," or "She gave me the creeps," or "I knew that would happen." These are some of the expressions that David and I think of as the body voice. They all express intuitive acceptance of our bodily-carried sense of personal truth.

We now know through research what we have always known intuitively. In America in the mid-20th century, Dr. Eugene Gendlin undertook a major research project looking into the question of what makes personal learning, emotional healing and change possible. He asked about how psychotherapy works. Why are some people able to use therapy to make change in their lives and others are not? The research team expected to find that some therapeutic methods worked better than others. They were surprised to discover that success had nothing at all to do with the skills or theoretical orientation of the therapist.

Gendlin discovered that body knowing is a crucial piece of awareness of self. The researchers found that they could predict failure in therapy from the very first session by checking to see if the client had the skill of looking within. They discovered that the clients' ability to connect to the body knowing is essential for success. Clients who did not have this capacity were unable to make change in therapy.

Focusing is a step-by-step process we use to teach people how to discover this critical skill and learn to use it. Gendlin's book *Focusing* was published in 1978. Since then it has become influential all over the world. It has been translated into seventeen languages and is taught in living rooms, community projects, changes groups and graduate schools, as well as by therapists.

We are all afraid of inner pain. This is why we are so tempted to avoid self-reflection. Focusing contributes new tools to transform our meditation practice. You no longer stay stuck in painful feelings. Your own bodily-held inner knowing will become a meaningful resource you can use, rather than something painful that you want to ignore or transcend. With NWM you will learn through your own experience that nothing in your inner world can actually hurt you. You will find that even if you become uncomfortable, the discomfort is only temporary.

Change is the essential nature of all human experiencing. The Buddha recognized this truth as the most important of his first principles: the impermanence of all things. He knew that negative feelings inevitably change, along with everything else. Focusing takes advantage of this natural tendency for change. Here you will discover that relief from inner pain comes naturally when feelings are fully experienced, even for just a few moments. Negative feelings such as tension and pain actually want to change and they will change when they are fully attended to. Here you will learn how to embrace the feeling and stay with it without fear and negative judgment. This is the power of letting it be exactly as it is. Letting-be lets it release and flow into some more comfortable form in the next new moment of constantly unfolding awareness.

What we experience as suffering can and will be transformed through the methods we teach here. There is no way we can avoid emotional pain from time to time, but now we have a way of healing. We are no longer captive to the chronic, ever-present agony of suffering. Merging body knowing with cognitive function brings all your resources together into a single stream of expanded awareness. This inclusive consciousness allows you to guide your life from a more evolved level.

New World Meditation

We begin with the practice of watching and counting your breaths. It is a simple practice that you can sustain on your own or with the support of a group, a therapist or a teacher. This practice works for us because following the breath brings body sensations and feelings directly into awareness. Ultimately, this brings your body back to life, filled with feeling and sensation, a source of pleasure and joy rather than pain and numbness.

You will learn how to acknowledge, honor and respect your feelings and issues exactly as they are. Feelings are valid just the way they are. This is a big leap, because we are so used to judging our feelings and trying to justify them. Deep inside you know exactly why you feel as you do. The path of emotional healing means discovering the source of your feelings, recognizing and honoring them as your personal truth. It is your personal truth that really matters. This is what you must rely upon to guide your life. Learning to drop judgment helps you to accept and embrace whatever you find inside. Simply recognize it and let it be.

Here is the secret of emotional healing: stuck feelings and internal pain are filled with seeds of change. You may sense a sort of anticipation, a tension or an edge in the feeling. When you follow it you will find something within that wants to be known. This following and staying with the feeling is the crux of the change process. You learn how to allow change to happen as you move through anxiety, restlessness and pain. On the other side you will find acceptance, relief and peace. Your body signals recognition of your inner truth by releasing and letting go of tension. In Focusing we call this a felt shift. It brings a completely new perspective.

Unconditional positive regard and non-judgmental acceptance are the essential ingredients of effective psychotherapy. In NWM you yourself provide these crucial qualities, allowing you to get out of the way of your built-in natural restorative process so that healing can happen. Emotional healing is fully integrated into your meditation practice. Relief from suffering becomes a reality.

Awakening is not the same as Enlightenment or awakening in the Buddhist sense, which is supremely difficult to achieve. The release of all attachments requires extreme sacrifice. Reaching Enlightenment requires many lifetimes. Monks enter the monastery in childhood and renounce the world, including property, family, sex and love. They work toward freeing themselves from attachment to all these things from the moment they enter the monastic life.

According to the Buddha our only hope of relief from suffering lies in letting go of all attachments, even to life itself. We use attachments to shelter us from impermanence, the constant fire of change and the reality of death. The denial of death is the ultimate attachment. It is masked by all the other myriad attachments we cling to, among them material things, youth and beauty. Even love is considered an attachment that leads to suffering, because when you love someone you immediately face the possibility of loss. The more precious the person becomes, the greater the threat.

Awakening in New World Meditation

The fruit of our practice is an Awakened Self, fully human, including body, self and soul. We believe that embracing our human condition, including our fears and limitations, our beauty, talents, creativity, all our feelings, leads to the highest happiness. Self-acceptance and self-forgiveness enables you to be stronger and more confident. You are relieved of anxiety and self-doubt and immensely more competent in meeting the challenges of life.

To abandon the body and the personal self is to deny the reality of our experience. In general, people who have no sense of self cannot function in the world. We think of them as mentally ill. This is why we believe it is impossible to release attachment to the self, the personal identity. Our practice is all about letting go of the false self, the persona we adopt when we cannot connect with our authentic desires and needs; our true nature that wants to be expressed. We can have a strong sense of individual identity and still be humble in our connection, and oneness with all humanity.

We honor the ancient wisdom of Buddhist thought, especially the truth of impermanence and the challenge of facing the reality of death. At the same time, what we learn from our practice changes our perspective on the nature of the self, as well as the inevitability of suffering. There will be pain from time to time, but suffering is not the essential nature of life. We know now that feelings can be reflected upon, injuries can be worked through and healed. They do not have to congeal and harden into suffering.

Through the Body/Mind Wisdom we rediscover and connect to our true selves, and recognize our deepest intentions. This secure inner knowing becomes our new default response, replacing the old struggle to figure out what others expect of us and how to please them. Now we guide our lives by making choices that feel good, rather than bad. Because empathy is alive in us, we feel bad when we act in a way that hurts others, and so we avoid it. This inner congruence, amazingly comfortable and secure, is our new personal reality. It comes with healing.

For us Nirvana is not a remote and unreachable dream. It is the reality of meditative ecstasy. In the stillness of meditation you float in a state of bliss, the ecstasy of joy and compassion. In that moment, which seems to last forever, the bliss of Nirvana is your reality. You truly feel no pain, no concern or worry. You are perfectly at peace. You are at one with the universe, no longer separate and alone, but connected to all things. This ecstasy is possible for you too.

Our view of love is a good example of this easier path. We agree that being willing to love is one of our ultimate challenges. Perhaps it is the most fearsome, because it brings the greatest joy. In loving there is so much to lose. But we are unwilling to give up love. On the contrary, we find that the blessing of true intimacy is made possible through the process of emotional healing.

Loving is worth the risk of loss. Through our own experience we have discovered that it is possible to recover from lost love and gain in wisdom and compassion. As you build confidence and learn to trust your own inner workings, you will find that you too have the strength to risk the joy of loving, as well as all the other wonderful possibilities of life. Your capacity for love expands as your heart continues to heal and open.

We believe the Buddha knew that Enlightenment is impossible without emotional healing. But he thought that healing could only be achieved through years of re-experiencing and confronting emotional pain again and again in meditation, until agony forces surrender. In surrender you finally accept impermanence, give up all attachment, and are relieved of suffering.

What we know today is that there is a shorter and less painful way to emotional healing. We now know that healing can be achieved only by clearly acknowledging the truth of personal reality, and finally coming to self-forgiveness. The Awakening we envision is an advanced consciousness and a high level of functioning that is pleasurable, satisfying, creative and productive. It is not a remote goal that takes 30, 3000, or 30,000 lives to reach. It is an Awakening you can aspire to reach, to live and to enjoy in this lifetime.

The ancient concept of compassion/wisdom, still lives in our new vision of the Awakened Self. It is the path that we see so very differently. Empathy gives birth to compassion when you see others as you see yourself. It is the realization of our full potential that makes it possible for us to reach the sweetness of compassion/wisdom, and awareness of the beauty and preciousness of all life, especially in the light of impermanence.

We honor your own unique inner wisdom. Only you know what is right for you. We each have the exclusive power and carry the whole responsibility for creating a life that is an expression of our true nature. It seems there is a unique trajectory that fits for each of us. Getting off-track, disconnecting from our deepest intentions, leads to negative outcomes: mistakes in judgment, false choices and unhappiness. In contrast, when you can stay connected to your true nature, your choices reflect that congruence, and you are happy, healthy and wise.

Only through the fully developed Body/Mind Wisdom, can we come to the complete realization of the Self, and stay connected with our true intentions. NWM is for those of us that choose to live in the world outside the monastery, with jobs and families. Our path is a way of life that inevitably leads to a new world, where we live in the fully developed consciousness of our true spiritual essence. This is the wonder of our full human potential.

Three

Self-Reflection and Self-Enquiry

New World Meditation is a continuing practice of self-reflection: always returning home to your essential self. With healing, you will be free to live from that central foundation, unencumbered by painful residue of the past. The journey of self-discovery is gentle and gradual. Success is about being rather than doing. It is important to be patient with your process, stay present in your body/mind and make room to welcome whatever might come to you. You don't need to struggle to gain insight; it will easily emerge in its own time. Your deeper self, in its wisdom, is always guiding your unfolding awareness.

Self-reflection and self-enquiry are essential to the whole process of healing and Awakening. They are the underlying foundation of change; the processes we rely upon for basic guidance all along the way.

Self-Reflection

All of Mindfulness is self-reflection, simply sitting with whatever you find within. The essence of self-reflection is a sort of nonjudgmental tracking, watching and witnessing your experience, noticing whatever comes up without trying to change it.

In self-reflection we adopt an attitude of gentle curiosity toward whatever we find inside.

We use a basic Mindfulness practice, following and counting the breaths, to bring your awareness into your body, and into the immediate. The body carries information in the form of sensations and feelings. They come to awareness as we follow the breath. Often they emerge together in the same moment. Sometimes thoughts come first; at other times you will first notice a body sense or feeling, and then notice the accompanying thought.

This is the body's voice. It will become your entry to the Body/Mind Wisdom. Your body voice becomes audible through daily practice. At first you will only momentarily hear it whisper. But each day that you sit in meditation you cultivate your ability to hear it more clearly, and reflect upon it, noticing and listening

With time in advanced practice the Body/Mind Wisdom will become your expanded consciousness, the reality of your ongoing experience. Now you will easily know what is right for you. In fact you won't be able to escape from your truth, because if you try to go against your true nature you will have an immediate sense of incongruence –something is not right –and you will instantly know what it is. This is the gift of expanded awareness you receive in advanced practice.

Yielding to the Flow

Experience unfolds in a constant dynamic of change. This flow is the very fabric of our existence. Like everything else, feelings are constantly changing; in fact they want to change. Nothing wants to remain static. We embrace the inescapable impermanence of all things. This includes everything: our personal experience of the continual unfolding of life, the material world and the entire universe.

The secret to success is yielding to the flow rather than trying to thwart it. This is the paradox: our first impulse is to try to get rid of whatever is bothering us. We naturally push away painful feelings. But trying to get rid of them only prolongs our pain and frustration. Trying to "get over it'" or "just forget about it" only keeps you stuck. You are fighting the natural and inevitable nature of change, and it simply won't work. You don't know it, but by pushing feelings away you are actually hanging on to pain, and with time it hardens into suffering.

There is a way that works for healing. Awareness always wants to move on. Every moment carries within it a certain tension, an edge that is pregnant with the next moment. The body always wants to return to a feeling of calm, which is release of stress. This is part of the body's natural force for healing. This "wanting to change" is especially strong for difficult feelings. The tension they carry puts pressure on them to morph into some form that is easier for the body to carry.

Simply give in, let it be, think of simply being with whatever is there. Surrender to whatever you find inside: happy, sad, hopeful. Your experience in this moment is your truth. Accept even your pain, your imperfections and faults just as they are. The feelings you think are unacceptable, like anger, hate, rage and envy come from a place inside that is hurting. Acknowledging this truth removes the sting of our faults and failures. This allows the body's natural healing tendency to work. Now you see yourself in the light of a new and more compassionate reality. We are all just human beings doing the best we can.

We know that you won't give up your usual way of judging your feelings until you are ready. For now, just know that you can and will relax when you accept your own personal pace of change, and begin to trust your inner process, the workings of your own body/mind. The decision to let go is made by your deepest self, in the inmost center of your being. Often you won't even notice the shift. It simply comes when you yield to the feeling; simply reflecting upon it instead of pushing it aside.

Once you can allow yourself to fully experience the feeling it will naturally flow into a more comfortable form. This is true of what we think is physical pain as well as what we recognize as emotional pain.

Negative judging is the opposite of yielding. It stands in the way of self-reflection. It takes attention away from your truth and directs it toward what is wrong with you, and how badly you feel about it. It is true that feelings can be very intense; they can make you quite uncomfortable, but they cannot kill you. Judging is a blind alley, a painful place that is hard to escape. It keeps you stuck in your old ways of feeling and thinking, and makes it impossible for you to enjoy your meditation or your life.

Nothing in nature is perfect. The idea that you need to be perfect or even pretend to be perfect is a cruel hoax. It is only an illusion that is keeping you stuck. You don't have to be perfect after all, and you never will be. Striving for perfection can only result in chronic long-term pain, the essence of suffering.

When you give up judging you are free to embark upon the path of self-reflection. As you practice facing your feelings you will come to the realization that they are not only harmless in the eyes of the curious and blameless witness, they are powerful guides. They point the way to deeper understanding. Only through this yielding can you open to receive the precious information that lives inside you: the meaning beneath your myriad memories, feelings and needs.

All your feelings are valid just as they are. It doesn't matter how you think you should feel, what is important is how you actually do feel. Your feelings come from a core of meaning that makes perfect sense in your experience, even when that perfect sense is yet to be revealed. Trust that this truth will eventually be clear to you. Feelings do not have to be logically justified. You don't need to spend time trying to decide whether you "should" feel the way you do. Trying to justify feelings is simply another instance of reliance on judging, hanging on to some preconceived idea of what is right or wrong.

True compassion means accepting and loving all your imperfections as part of your beauty. You are just a regular person after all. As you look around you can't help but realize that we are all the same; our imperfections are simply a part of the human condition, our shared reality.

It may encourage you to remember that every ingredient you need to change your life is right here, already inside you, just waiting for your loving attention. You will realize that some of your familiar ways of behaving or viewing the world are no longer working. Memories will resurface as your meditation deepens. Now you can review these memories without judging, give up self-blame and self-hate, open your heart and feel the return of loving energy. Along the way you will gain the freedom to make wiser choices, shaped by self-compassion instead of self-criticism.

Self-Enquiry

As we sit in meditation, we are always streaming the input of daily experience. Unresolved events of the day come to mind. In self-reflection, we feel the wanting to know. This wanting will become familiar until we recognize it immediately. It is a driving curiosity. Here is some feeling quality, some emotional loading: a flavor that compels our attention. It draws us to sit with this experience for a time. Memories emerge to be reclaimed, deciphered and understood.

At first this unfolding will seem mysterious. We wonder where this particular memory came from, and what it is about today's event, and all that it evokes, that now brings it to awareness. This wondering is another ingredient of the healing process, inherent in the nature of self-enquiry.

New World Meditation includes a proactive process of self-enquiry. This is what makes it unique and so much more powerful, faster and easier than Mindfulness practice alone. Self-enquiry goes beyond self-reflection to ask for more information from the feeling/sensation/thought. We have special ways of asking that come from the Focusing process. The most powerful of these is what we call felt sensing. It is a way of going beneath the sensation/emotion to access a far bigger knowing, vastly more complex and multi-faceted, filled with meaning and pointing toward your truth and what you need most. Often, simply getting clear on what you feel is sufficient for resolution and release of tension. Other times you will discover actions that you need to take. As we continue we will expand upon felt sensing as a tool for self-enquiry. It is especially important in the phases of emotional healing in advanced practice.

In self-enquiry we take yielding even further; proactively moving toward the feeling. Learning to lean into difficult feelings allows you to take advantage of the healing flow. This seems counterintuitive, but it is how change and healing happen. It is what works. Whatever you carry inside cannot change until it is fully experienced. (Gendlin, 1978)

The steps of New World Meditation are based on these principles of self-inquiry and self-reflection. We will show you how to apply them in meeting all that you experience, in meditation and in daily life. Mastering the tools we present here will make it easier for you to move through and release the inevitable interruptions and to sustain your meditation, eventually relaxing into the inner peace of your true nature. You will progress toward Awakening through continuing practice, gradually coming to peace with all that you are and building a more authentic life. You will feel the deep sense of security that comes only with self-acceptance. Through this healing practice you will open your heart to compassion/wisdom. This heart opening comes with the blessing of self-forgiveness, allowing compassion to flow freely from your heart to all of who you are.

Four

The Seven Steps
of New World Meditation

STEP 1: Make a decision to sit still for 15 minutes or more.

STEP 2: Turn your attention inward, bringing awareness into your body. Begin to track and count your breaths, from 1 to 10, over and over.

STEP 3: Encounter the interruptions, whatever it is that takes your awareness away from the breath. Notice each one with non-judgmental witnessing, and allow it to fade out of awareness.

STEP 4: If it did not fade away, but is only a thought, without emotional loading, gently put it aside for right now.

STEP 5: With emotionally-loaded interruptions, what we call the "graspings," those that will not be put aside, hold whatever comes in caring loving presence, and receive any information or insight you find there. You will know this step is complete when you can gently put it aside.

STEP 6: Remember to return to the breath. Follow your breath as you inhale and exhale, and resume counting.

STEP 7: Enjoy the clear space, and experience your true nature.

The process of NWM is cyclical and grounded in the core rhythm of the breath, to which you will return again and again. Interruptions—anxiety, restlessness, thoughts and/or feelings—will come up and you will temporarily forget and drift away. The interruption will let go when it has received sufficient attention. You initiate a new cycle (steps 3 through 6) every time you return to your breath. Drifting away is a normal part of the process; it is the returning that is most important.

Every session of meditation is different, shaped by your own unique process. But the direction of your awareness is always deepening toward the center of your body/mind, the still, clear space deep inside. With each cycle you are progressively letting go of stress that has been holding on in your body, so your breathing will gradually deepen and body sensation will change. The seven steps are only an outline of the experience; each step will be explained in detail as we continue.

We have been inspired by Sogyal Rinpoche, author of the *Tibetan Book of Living and Dying* (Rinpoche, S. 1993), which describes three stages of all meditation: come home to yourself, release the graspings, and relax in your nature. The seven steps of NWM correspond beautifully with these stages.

Stage One/Steps 1 & 2 – Come Home to Yourself

Meditation begins when you decide to close your eyes and sit quietly for a few minutes. By letting go of external stimuli you automatically turn your attention inward. This is meditation: simply experiencing your inner self as you are in this moment.

Now begin to count your breaths from 1 to 10 over and over: a full inhale and exhale counts as one breath. As you track your breath, the filling and emptying, you are coming home to your body. Notice how you are breathing in the moment, whether your breathing is shallow or deep, full or restricted. Notice all the different sensations in your chest and stomach. Don't try to change your breathing, or the sensations you feel, just allow it to be whatever it is right now.

Stage Two/Steps 3, 4, 5, & 6: Release the Graspings

In NWM we invite the inner self to speak by the simple act of sitting to meditate. As we count our breaths, thoughts and feelings come spontaneously. They can be simple or complex, trivial or loaded with feeling that implies great meaning. As we sit in silence we can't help musing upon life's events. Some of these musings are simply thoughts, easily set aside for now. Others come with attention-grabbing bodily-carried feelings. These are the ones that we think of as graspings rather than simple interruptions.

Interruptions

At the beginning of stage two (step 3) you will notice simple transitory and incidental distractions, such as sounds from outside the room, or the temperature of the air on your skin. Stray thoughts and unimportant events of the day then come to mind. You might remember that you have to stop at the store for something needed in the house. These distractions usually fade as soon as you notice them. Simply acknowledging them gives them sufficient recognition and they easily float away. If they don't float off, simply set them aside for now. Imagine taking that thought, wrapping it all up and putting it down on a table or on the floor next to you. Experiment until you find an image that works for you. David imagines a box next to him where he puts things that don't seem important but are acting as chatter in his mind. Promising to handle it later will often satisfy.

When you acknowledge something and are able to set it aside you will find that it is no longer carried in body sensation. It has been given the attention it needs for now, and you automatically remember to return to your breath. Often you won't know exactly why the thought is no longer clinging to you. It is simply not as compelling.

It is normal to experience a seemingly continuous stream of interruptions, gradually declining in frequency until they finally fade out completely. The flow of interruptions and graspings is the way your organism is healing itself by offloading stressors. You don't need to worry that you will get lost and forget to count your breaths. Drifting off into thoughts or feelings is normal and it is only temporary. It happens when the interruptions and/or graspings come up to pull your attention away from the breath. The signal to return to the breath is noticing you have forgotten to keep track. If you can't remember where you left off, simply begin again with the number one.

The Graspings

As minor, unimportant things move aside, more significant thoughts and issues emerge. They often carry not only a thought, but a bodily sensation or feeling. It could be any kind of emotion, even painful feelings such as anxiety, anger, hurt or fear. They are issues that have meaning in your life and remain unresolved. These sticky issues and feelings are the graspings: they tend to keep hanging on because they have something to tell you. The extra time you spend with these issues will benefit you greatly. You will gain new insight into their meaning and significance.

Simply stay with self-reflection at first, accepting whatever comes and allowing it to speak. Some of these graspings respond to deep acknowledgment. For instance, admitting how anxious you are about an upcoming court date may be all that is needed for the anxiety to decrease and for you to be able to put it aside for now.

Graspings come in two basic forms, sensations/emotions or words. Sometimes they come together. If you get a thought alone, check to see if it connects with a sensation. When a bodily-carried feeling comes up, you may hear your inner voice whisper something, or perhaps an image will appear in your mind's eye. If you get a sensation first, and no thought or image immediately comes, ask yourself what this is about in your life. You may recognize it, or it may remain a mystery.

In self-enquiry we use the tools of Focusing to maximize the healing potential of our daily practice. Here we are using the word healing to mean resolving inner conflict, which allows us to return to the breath. With Focusing we exponentially increase the speed and efficiency of this process. This gives you a more satisfying experience in daily practice because you will have a way to get to the bliss of the clear space more easily and quickly.

In order to explore and resolve complex feeling-loaded issues we must first sit with them, getting a sense of them in a curious and friendly way. We acknowledge them with close attention. We listen inside and allow them to speak. Then we inquire into their source, and explore our own motivations. What is this feeling about? Where in me, or in my life, does it come from? Sometimes this process of concentrated attention and deep acknowledgment allows them to let go. Other times they reveal new information, things about ourselves that we were not aware of. We will sometimes uncover memories from the past we have not thought about for years, or gain insight into our blind spots: places in us that are stuck in old dysfunctional patterns. This is valuable insight. The stuck spots are most often the result of old patterns, ways we used to cope with hurtful events. Now we see the hurt and can deal with the injury in a more effective way.

What is most important is the quality of attention you offer the feeling. Acknowledging it, recognizing it and honoring it means validating it and owning it as your own. Staying present with it for whatever time it needs is part of the owning. You are admitting that this is how you feel, even though you might wish you felt differently.

Remember to use the attitude of caring loving presence with any feeling/thought that makes you uncomfortable. Caring loving presence means gently holding the issue in awareness as you would a small child that is in pain. Imagine holding a distressed baby in your arms. The baby doesn't have words, but you can convey comfort through your body, the tender way you hold her, and your loving eye contact as well as the soothing tone of your voice. This is the attitude of caring loving presence, which you will find so very helpful when you meet up with your own inner distress.

Acknowledgement and acceptance is what allows the feeling to let go for right now. Yes, I do feel that way and I accept that. Your body releases it and you can move on. You may not be finished with it, but you know what it is and can revisit it at a later time. You will then return to the breath.

Trust your body. Remember that the feeling, whatever it is, will only hold on as long as it needs attention. Once you get its message, it releases and allows you to return to the breath. It automatically takes all the time it needs before receding from awareness. You don't need to be concerned about possibly wasting time on feelings that are not important. If the feeling does not want to let go, you know that it has more meaning that it wants to convey. Trust that, too, and simply continue listening and feeling about it, sitting with it and allowing it to speak. Sometimes you will need to promise the issue or feeling that you will spend more time with it the next morning.

Stage 3/Step 7: Relax In Your Nature

One way of imagining this stage is by visualizing the mind as a pond. Thoughts and feelings drop into the pond like pebbles falling into water, and ripples emanate from each thought. As you gently acknowledge and set aside each pebble you will see fewer ripples in the water. This clearing of the pond seems to happen all by itself as you pass through stage two and flow into stage three.

Reaching stage three is very rewarding. When all of your immediate concerns have been set aside, you reach an experience of deep rest, leaving you refreshed and renewed. In this space there are moments of no sound, and even no breath. This is the ecstatic bliss of emptiness described by experienced meditators. This is often referred to as the clear field of mind. David and I have reached this blissful space many times, and it is profoundly satisfying. Even coming into this state for a few seconds makes a lasting impression.

How long should it take you to pass through releasing the graspings? Most people need to establish a daily practice and maintain it for a few months before they can pass through the graspings and go on into stage three. There are always new issues, along with more significant long-term stressors. The skills you are using are new to you, and you will need time to master them.

Everyone is different and some days we need more time. I often reach a clear space of blissful peace after 30 to 40 minutes, although it is easy for me to spend an hour or even more. If you are a beginning meditator it will probably take longer than 30 to 40 minutes, just as it will if it has been several days since you had an opportunity to meditate.

Here the concept of nonattachment is useful. Think of simply doing the process as it is explained, without concern about the outcome. The experience of the clear space is a gift that you will not always receive. We have no "goal"; the process of meditation unfolds the way it will. Often you will go through your meditation and never reach the clear space. You haven't done anything wrong. Maybe you have a lot on your mind today, much to explore and understand.

You will often reach a state of peace without actually solving any problem that may emerge. Through dropping judgment and opening yourself to fully experience your feelings, the nature of the problem often changes, so that you will no longer feel it in the same way. What you thought of as a problem is not a problem at all. It may be something you want to spend more time with, but you will no longer carry it with such intensity. You are resolving inner conflict.

Catching up With the Backlog

Beginning meditation practice is an invitation to your inner self to bring up whatever is unfinished in your past or your current life. At times you will feel flooded with concerns, as though you are opening the door to an overstuffed closet. As you repeat your meditation practice on a daily basis, you will gradually clean the closet, sorting and processing all that you find inside.

When you first begin to meditate you can expect to have a backlog, a buildup of unattended thoughts and feelings. Some are superficial incidentals of everyday life, while others are significant themes that will keep returning. At first you may experience these graspings as an irritation or even a torment. Eventually they will become familiar to you, and hopefully you will learn to greet them like old friends: "Oh, there you are again, still with me."

The flow of NWM is always moving forward, even when that movement is not obvious to you. As you learn to use our tools you will come to see more significant interruptions as an asset rather than as an annoyance, and your meditation time will be more comfortable for you. You will feel wonderful when you have attended to whatever is there, so that it moves aside and you can relax in peaceful bliss.

New World Mediation honors your own personal rhythm. Whatever arises in you will stay in awareness only until its need for attention and acknowledgement is met. NWM provides support for staying with whatever comes by encouraging you to experiment with letting go of judging. The deeper meaning, the message carried within your feelings, naturally wants to come out into awareness but may need more time.

The Stages of Meditation Unfold Naturally

Gradually, with regular practice and sufficient time you will be able to let go of more and more thoughts and worries. Your mind is progressively quieting. The stages unfold naturally and effortlessly in the flow of your meditative awareness. You won't even notice transitions between stages.

As you repeat the cycle you will feel as though your chest has expanded and you have more free space in which to breathe. Your breathing and other body sensations will change, because with each cycle you are progressively letting go of tension and stress. At some point you may experience a rush of endorphins in your brain, a spreading sense of relaxation and warmth through your body. This release seems to happen after several cycles, as the graspings are beginning to slow down and you feel more peaceful.

As we continue, you will see that NWM offers you not just a momentary escape from life's pain, but an actual healing of whatever is causing that pain. Daily practice will continuously improve your quality of life and build your self-esteem.

PART TWO:
BUILDING A DAILY PRACTICE

Five

Daily Practice

When you meditate on a daily basis you will be generally calmer, your thinking will be clarified and you will be more capable of staying in the present moment as you live through your day. Your habit of regular meditation increases your capacity to sustain concentration, which will maximize your potential in your work or study, or in any creative process.

There is a big difference between meditating occasionally and sustaining a daily practice. When you meditate only once in a while you spend most of your time clearing everyday concerns and distractions. In contrast, daily practice initiates a continuing process of insight, healing and expanding awareness. To begin and continue healing, all you have to do is show up for meditation every morning.

When you establish a daily practice you awaken a healing force within you that has its own energy. It wants to keep moving. The power of intention is well known. Deciding to establish a regular practice is making a commitment. It means setting your intention to be present each day for you, available to listen to your deepest self, using the skills that you learn in this book.

There will be times when you will miss a day, or a few days. You may be traveling, or have a cold, or need to get to work early. Don't be hard on yourself. As you gradually strengthen your habit of daily practice, it will be easier to take this time for yourself. When you miss a day, just resume the following morning.

I recommend that you meditate in the morning. This way you will experience maximum benefit all day. Most of us have a long-established morning routine we started in childhood. Parents work hard to help us cement the morning ritual because it is so important to getting along in the world. Changing any long-established habit pattern is very difficult. When you think about it this way you can see that finding a time and building a habit of morning meditation is not easy.

A habit is created when we repeat a behavior many times until it is familiar and comfortable. After many repetitions, sequences of behaviors engrave a pattern of synaptic firings in the brain; you might compare it to a tattoo. Once such a pattern is established it becomes resistant to change. Until recently we thought that habit patterns were fixed permanently in the brain. Now we have research proving that the brain has a quality of plasticity enabling it to adapt, to alter old patterns and generate new ones as the need arises. (Siegel, 2007)

It requires systematic repetition to create an enduring habit. To establish a daily practice you simply need to sit in meditation for fifteen minutes consecutive mornings for as few as 18 days. On average it takes 66 days to establish a habit, but everyone is different. Habits developed by this method operate almost automatically. After this initial period you will feel uncomfortable if you don't meditate in the morning. This is the easiest way I know to begin and strengthen your routine of daily practice. The rewards of meditation make establishing a daily practice much easier.

Choose a time in the morning when there is a natural transition. You might decide to meditate right after you wash your face, brush your teeth and are fully awake, but not yet dressed for the day. Experiment with different times until you find one that feels good. Some people want to have a cup of tea or coffee before they begin.

Creating a Personal Ritual

A personal ritual reinforces and supports your daily practice. A ritual builds a series of associations that remind your brain of the altered state you are about to enter. The ritual actually begins your transition into meditation. To create a ritual that feels good, try some or all of the following: meditating at the same time every morning, wearing the same robe or the same sweatshirt, sitting in the same place, assuming the same posture.

The more senses you can involve in your ritual, the more securely the habit will be ingrained in your neural pathways. Consider the use of incense. Smell is processed in the most primitive part of the brain, so it is a powerful reminder. Find a variety that is especially pleasurable to you. The scent will become a familiar path inward, so that even when you are nervous or upset it will calm you and help you to begin meditation. With time the ritual will take on the same comforting feeling as meditation itself.

Here is another idea of how a ritual could go. You might build a simple altar. For a while I used a tray, which I placed on the floor directly in front of my sitting place. You could gather a few small objects that symbolize qualities or experiences you wish to cultivate. You might pick a single blossom from the garden and place it in a vase directly in front of you as a reminder of the beauty of nature. As you slowly close your eyes, the last cue you see is this little flower. In this way, the picking of the flower begins the process of floating inward, and can become a sweet moment of relaxing into your quiet time. You can make your ritual as simple or as elaborate as you like.

There are many ways to sit in meditation. You will find a way that feels right for you. I remember seeing a painting of a Buddhist monk at the Japanese art museum. He was seated on the floor, facing the wall as if to shut out the world, symbolizing turning inward. This is something I tried for a while, it worked for me and I enjoyed it.

For years I sat cross legged on the floor, but over time my knees began to complain. Now I sit in a chair. The important thing is to keep your spine as straight as possible. There is nothing wrong with having a pillow for your back. If you are using a chair, choose one in which you can arrange support so that you can sit straight, both feet on the floor and hands resting in your lap. If you are sitting on the floor use a firm pillow to support your buttocks. Sit on the front edge of the pillow. You will find that by moving your pelvis forward, it will tilt more comfortably toward the floor and you will be able to sit with your spine straight with little effort. If you need support for your back while sitting on the floor it is easy to sit in front of a chair or sofa.

You can sit anywhere to meditate. The important part is finding a place where you are comfortable, and then sitting in that same place each morning. Start by walking through your home, considering different places where you might enjoy meditating. Look for a spot that feels safe, private, quiet, and comfortable. This is an important part of the process, so take a few minutes just for this phase.

When you find a place that seems right, try it out. Before you sit down, turn off the phone and close the door, to ensure that the environment is quiet and you won't be interrupted. Closing the door becomes part of your ritual; you are creating a safe space that will help you to relax. Sit quietly in your new place, and move around until you feel comfortable. If you are using a chair, put both feet on the floor rather than crossing your legs or ankles. Settle your hands into your lap. Close your eyes and give yourself several minutes to relax into your body. Allow the chair or the floor to support you. Get the idea that there is nothing you need to do right now. Notice the weight of your body against the chair or the pillow, and the pressure of your feet on the floor. Begin to track your breath as you inhale and exhale, counting your breath from 1 to 10 over and over.

You may have trouble meditating for more than 5 minutes when you first begin practice. Maybe you are uneasy about feelings or thoughts that could come up, or afraid that you won't be able to sit still. It is fine to begin with 5 or 7 minutes. You will be surprised at how fast the time goes. I suggest beginning with a short time and increasing to 15 minutes, and then 20 minutes or more.

Most of the people I have trained enjoy their meditation right from the start. Five minutes pass very quickly and they discover that they soon move on to a longer time. When you pass the 20 minute mark, forget the clock and meditate as long as you want. For me it is a treat to meditate for an hour or more. Don't set any expectation for how long you will meditate beyond 5 minutes, and then just continue for as long as you like.

Notice the feeling that comes in your body as you go within. Check out how it feels to meditate in this place. You may have both positive and negative feelings. Open yourself to welcome any new awareness without judging. When you are finished, spend some time reflecting upon how this first try felt for you and take a few moments to notice and appreciate any good feelings you have inside as you look forward to your new practice. You might want to take a few notes in your journal. If you don't have a personal journal, I hope you will consider getting one. It can be quite helpful to take a few notes after meditating. Sometimes important thoughts and ideas come during meditation.

Sitting down to meditate is all you need to do. You are inviting your inner self to speak. The flow of unfolding awareness begins as soon as you come into your body and start to follow your breath. Your daily practice is so simple, and yet it is such a profound force for change and for peace of mind.

The self-discipline of daily practice builds personal power. Returning to your breath over and over strengthens your power to set an intention and follow through, building self-esteem. It is the returning itself that is important. This is the key discipline that is so empowering. You will encounter more intense feelings and memories as your practice progresses. The strength you build in beginning practice will give you the confidence to meet these more intense interruptions, and take full advantage of their healing potential.

Six

Reclaiming the Body

We believe that emotional healing is the only path to Awakening. Only through a healing journey can we reach the stage of self-forgiveness, essential for the empathy and compassion that define Enlightenment. Reclaiming the body with all its feelings and memories is a key part of this healing journey. Let us explain why this is true.

Process Skipping

Process skipping is a term we are using to talk about the many ways we avoid our difficult feelings. The reason is obvious. We are afraid of our pain, guilt and shame. We want to skip over the direct experience of remembering painful feelings because we know it will hurt all over again.

Feelings are carried in the body. The body has its own voice; it speaks in tightness, warmth, expansion, contraction, coolness, heaviness and lightness. Body sensation and emotion are always there in the background of our thoughts, signaling our feelings: sadness, grief, anger and hurt, along with happiness, pleasure, joy and excitement. The only way we can avoid all our feelings is to abandon the body and numb out. Many of us defend against our inner pain by ignoring the body voice and withdrawing awareness from the body itself. Some people have intentionally or unconsciously numbed out their body for so long that they no longer feel any sensation below the neck.

The process we want to skip turns out to be healing itself. We are so afraid of our feelings that we hold them inside, continuing to suffer. We are afraid to live through the stages of change described in chapter 4: spending time experiencing whatever it is, acknowledging it in a nonjudgmental way and accepting it as our truth. These are the crucial steps of change that let the feeling move through the body and be relieved. By pushing our pain out of awareness we are hanging on to our suffering.

Recently I read a book by a woman who is a meditation teacher. She writes of her journey of suffering and Awakening. For eleven years she lived in a spiritual community, dedicated herself to meditation and was married to a man in the group. Unfortunately the path she was on taught her to ignore her feelings. This teaching was a dead-end because it offered no way of accessing the bodily-carried knowing that we call the Body/Mind Wisdom. She was immersed in a spiritual life, yet she was suffering every day, unhappy in her marriage and her life style. She found no real comfort, insight or healing in her meditation practice.

She was stuck for eleven years in a fruitless search for Enlightenment, continuing to suffer from emotional pain because of the error of process skipping. She hoped, perhaps she believed, that she could attain advanced consciousness without dealing with her feelings, the realm of the body. In order to sustain her life style she had to ignore and suppress her deep bodily-carried sense of personal truth.

Finally, she discovered Focusing and began working with the felt sense, Gendlin's term for the body knowing. She acknowledged her suffering, and grew in strength as she used her Focusing skills to connect with her deeper, more authentic self. Ultimately, she left the community, divorced her husband and started a whole new life. By reclaiming her body and her own personal truth, she was able to heal.

Process skipping begins when parents don't know how to deal with our feelings, so they tell us to go away. They repeat what their parents told them: big boys don't cry, stop feeling sorry for yourself, stop pouting, shut up or I'll give you something to cry about. The suffering of our parents is carried on to us. Our anger, hurt and sadness rekindle the pain of their own ignored and abandoned inner child. They remind our parents of their own suffering. This is why they can't tolerate our feelings. They can only teach us their own ways, the old pattern of closing down feelings and numbing out the body.

What we usually think of as growing-up means giving up your inconvenient feelings and getting on with the work of life. We internalize the critical voice of mother/father, and it continues to play in our heads. We learn process skipping by example. We watch our parents avoid their own feelings and we buy into it. We tell ourselves to get over it and keep a stiff upper lip. We learn that crying means feeling sorry for yourself, and shows weakness and self-pity.

Thinking Our Way to Emotional Health

Many pop-psych books promise optimal mental health the easy way, without confronting your feelings and emotional wounds. One popular approach teaches that all you have to do is change your thoughts and you change your life. It is very appealing because thoughts emanate from the prefrontal cortex of the brain and are under conscious control.

Positive thinking can work for you if you have no real emotional wounds. Affirmations make you feel better; they stimulate ideas and different ways of thinking about your problems. But positive thinking is not a tool for healing emotional wounds or changing deeply ingrained ways of viewing the world.

One client I worked with had an episode of major depression and was treated "successfully" with cognitive behavioral therapy. He was able to get out of bed and go back to his life and work. Eight years later he realized that he continued to suffer the pain of the original wound. He had never really recovered. The therapy "worked" but was simply a Band-Aid. It allowed him to function, but he was still suffering. He was lonely and depressed, unable to establish a lasting intimate relationship.

Powerful painful feelings cannot be disposed of through reprogramming or simply deciding to change them. This is the truth we don't want to face. Thoughts originate in the prefrontal cortex of the brain, while emotions and emotionally-loaded memories are stored and processed in the midbrain, not fully available to conscious reasoning. This is why we cannot think our way to feeling good.

Too many gurus in the West promise Enlightenment the easy way. They gain popularity by teaching disciples to bypass feelings and emotional pain, split off, detach from the body and float off into fantasy and imagery. It feels good because you leave all your cares behind. Intense and colorful imagery is new, exciting and entertaining and you want to believe that this is the doorway to Nirvana. This is entertainment and relaxation, but not a way of healing or a path to Enlightenment.

The trouble is that when this type of meditation ends, and you go back to your life, you realize that nothing has changed. Your problems remain the same. You have pleasurably passed the time, but suffering returns. Many people give up meditating when they see that nothing in their life has changed for the better.

Thinking we can transcend the body and leave it completely behind is an error shared by many teachers and meditators all over the world. This approach actually turns off thoughtful intelligent people. They know intuitively that there must be more to the journey; Awakening can't come that easily. Repulsed by what they see as phony faith healing, they close their minds to the tremendous benefits of daily practice. This is a loss for them and for the community of seekers.

Before we can change anything in our lives we must take a clear look at what needs changing: our feelings and whatever gave rise to them. Then we can begin on a new healing path that will ultimately bring a better life. No matter how process skipping is used, it works against change and blocks progress. It is basically self-protective. It shelters us from our feelings but keeps us from even considering what is really going on.

Process skipping keeps us going through the motions, but we remain crippled. It becomes a way of life. Process skipping blocks self-enquiry, so we stay the same: stuck with our mistakes, our poor choices and our repeated patterns of self-destructive behavior.

Numbing Out

If we are not to feel our feelings, what will we do with them? We begin by simply telling them to shut up and leave us alone. We progress to ignoring them and finally to numbing out: a dangerous and destructive process of erasing body sensation from consciousness.

Feelings are composed of energy. Often we feel them in the body center, the chest and stomach, but they actually affect the entire body. You might think of the body as a tube-shaped balloon filled with air. When you squeeze one end the other end gets bigger. Feelings, like air in the balloon, don't go away. When not acknowledged, the energy of the feeling cannot be processed; it must be stored somewhere your body.

The body remembers. You fight down your tears and suppress your anger and hurt and you think the feeling is gone. You no longer experience it so it must be over. But ignored and neglected feelings live on, stored in your tissues, muscles and organs, in the form of pain, tension, constriction and reduced circulation. And there they will remain, and go on undermining your health, until they are brought to consciousness, acknowledged and resolved.

Leading medical experts estimate that 90% of disease is caused or complicated by stress. This epidemic of stress is a strong contributor to both high medical costs and poor medical outcomes (The Congressional Prevention Coalition on Stress Prevention: Its Impact on Health and Medical Savings, 1998). This was a surprise even to me. Although I knew that many illnesses and diseases were aggravated by stress, the word "cause" in a scientific context implies a probability so high as to establish certainty. Stress not only contributes to disease but is the source of it. The emotional pain of neglected and ignored feelings is a form of physiological stress which manifests in fear, anxiety, worry, sleep disturbance, emotional pain and chronic ongoing physiological arousal, with all its negative consequences, such as adrenal depletion and reduced immune function.

The numbness we use to ward off emotional pain plants seeds of illness that become real medical threats. A destructive cycle is set in motion: we feel the pain, we want to avoid it, and so we block body sensation out of awareness. You don't even realize that you are avoiding your feelings, because the habit started so early and it is so embedded. Stress progresses unnoticed, eventually causing illness and disease.

There are three degrees of numbness noticed by therapists who are aware of our divorce from the body. For some people the body is simply a physical object that serves as support for the head. These people experience the body as a machine, a distant object rather than part of the living self. Other people have a greater degree of body awareness; they experience sensations in the body but they have no idea that they could be connected to feelings. A third group have awareness in the body; they recognize that body sensation carries feelings, but they don't know what to do with what they experience, how to make sense of it and gain insight into its meaning.

Ask yourself where you fit in. Maybe you need additional help in reconnecting with body experience. I suggest you pause, take five minutes several times a day to simply check in with your body. Find a time and place where you can be alone and undisturbed. Bring awareness into your chest, stomach and belly. Just notice what you are experiencing. You don't need to change or fix anything. Simply notice what is happening in that moment and relax as you breathe. Then return to whatever you were doing. This relaxation and body awareness exercise is very effective in helping you become more aware of what is going on inside. It will reduce stress and improve health while it energizes your meditation practice.

The Way of New World Meditation

Our new method makes process skipping unnecessary, and allows you to make peace with the hurt of the past. We are born with feelings, but what we do with them is learned. Just as old habits can be changed, we can relearn a more effective ways to deal with our feelings. In NWM we learn that the way to change difficult feelings is through acknowledging them and staying present with them long enough to allow them to change. After all, change is the natural flow of all of our experience. Now process skipping is no longer our only refuge from suffering.

This is a meditation practice, but it is also a process of emotional healing. When you reclaim your body, you activate the natural healing energy of the human organism. Once liberated it wants to continue. In re-owning the body and re-owning your feelings you are beginning the healing journey. This is the first step in the healing journey. Eventually it will bring you to self-forgiveness and self-acceptance, inner peace, mental health and finally to Awakening.

Seven

Demystifying Resistance

Keeping your commitment to yourself is the crucial self-discipline that empowers you and builds confidence. Each day that you keep your commitment to meditation you are building your inner strength. Yet most of us have trouble meditating daily, at least in early practice. The reason for this is resistance, based on fear. As your practice evolves and matures you can't help but encounter powerful feelings and memories and the ache of unmet needs. These strong feelings trigger restlessness, easy distraction and other symptoms. Resistance is completely normal and to be expected. It usually surfaces as soon as you begin daily practice, when you turn attention inward, or even think about meditating. It is especially active in stage two: Release the Graspings.

It is sadly ironic that we resist our own intentions, when we ourselves decided to undertake a regular practice. But it is only natural that we are afraid of our painful feelings. For years we have found ways of avoiding them, and those habits don't just dissolve and go away.

Resistance feeds off our fear of the unknown. You don't really know what feelings and memories might be there inside, what you will encounter as the journey deepens. You might even be afraid that meditation will change you in some unknown way. I want to reassure you that your core self will be strengthened through your practice and you will feel more comfortable in being fully authentic.

The key to disarming resistance is recognizing it for what it is. Once you understand the many ways it manifests you can turn it to your advantage to gain insight and speed your progress. Resistance takes many forms, the most obvious of which is finding a reason not to meditate today. You might think you are too busy or have more urgent things to do. These thoughts can be a sign that there is some feeling you want to avoid. When you are anxious it is particularly tempting to put off sitting because getting quiet brings the anxiety and the feeling underneath it directly into awareness. When you respond to anxiety by avoiding meditation, you defeat your own best interest. Meditation is the very medicine you need to move through the anxiety and relax.

Once you are actually meditating, resistance manifests through a variety of symptoms. It can masquerade so that you are unconscious of what is really going on. For example, you may not recognize physical discomfort and restlessness as resistance. You might feel like getting up, leaving the room and giving up on meditation for today. But you made a commitment to yourself that is truly important. When you move around you are acting against your promise to sit still and be with yourself for a defined time.

Restlessness is one of the most common forms of resistance. Your ability to overcome restlessness will grow rapidly in the first few weeks of your practice.

Working Through Resistance

Rather than fighting your resistance and blaming yourself for having it, you will learn to accept it and use it for greater self-understanding. It is the same as anything else you encounter in your inner world. You have nothing to fear in sitting with it and being curious about it. What is this restlessness? Why is it coming up now? Allow yourself to feel it completely for a few moments without yielding to the impulse to move. You will discover something more under it. This is the opening to relief.

By withdrawing negative judgment, you can see your resistance in a new and brighter light. Whatever it is that comes up, ask inside what it might be about. With this open question you are inviting it to speak. You may be surprised by the answer. You may even hear your inner voice whisper that something is coming up, some new awareness that makes you uncomfortable, and you would rather avoid it. It is perfectly acceptable, understandable and normal for you to be afraid of the feeling. Whatever comes, simply acknowledge it, and let it be. Admitting the truth will always be a relief.

We all have our own habitual patterns of resistance. You will soon be on familiar terms with your own favorites. As soon as you acknowledge the pattern, the feelings that lie under it will be revealed. Your willingness to blamelessly witness whatever emerges is the key to progress.

There are two important changes in consciousness that you need to make in order to deal with your resistance in a positive way. First, and most importantly, remind yourself yet again of the need to release any wish you might have to scold yourself about your own difficulties in starting your practice. Many of us have a pervasive habit of self-criticism. As you sit down to meditate, dedicate yourself to nonjudgmental witnessing. This is a transformational shift in consciousness that you will be cultivating all along the path.

Secondly, realize that you are in charge of yourself. Your intention to heal and advance in consciousness is stronger than any momentary impulse. Choose to take your power, accept your resistance, explore and resolve it so that you can do what you want in life, not simply in meditation but in any endeavor you choose.

Recall the method of gentle curiosity and acknowledgment we introduced in chapter 4. Then use the process, honoring and respecting your resistance and then asking it to step aside for right now, just as you would any interruption during meditation. Your resistance will release its hold when you identify and name the feeling underneath it..

Common Forms of Resistance

Rationalizing is resistance disguised as nice logical reasons why you don't need/want to meditate today. These thoughts seem to make perfect sense. I used to think about all the phone calls I had to make and emails I needed to write. They seemed urgent at the time, but it was just an excuse for not keeping my promise. Rationalization is easily recognized by its purely mental nature. Listening to the reasonable voice of avoidance is an easy way out of feeling, but it won't help you to progress.

Most of my professional colleagues, psychologists and psychotherapists, meditate regularly. They find it helpful in sustaining optimal functioning in all realms of life. There are a few who report they have given up trying to sit still to meditate even for ten or fifteen minutes. As soon as they encounter any anxiety or restlessness they give in to it. Instead of continuing their meditation they do yoga or go for walks. They rationalize that these activities are just as effective as regular sitting meditation. In reality, nothing could be more important than beginning your day with sitting practice, centering and connecting with you.

My friends' reasons are only rationalizations. Sitting in meditation is the only activity that brings to your attention the immediate and direct experience of your inner world. Sitting is the fastest way you will be confronted with your resistance and have the chance to explore its meaning. You will recognize the truth of this as you continue learning this practice.

Most meditators find that they have the problem of postponing meditation. I know from personal experience that sitting is most effective early in the morning, yet it is so easy to tell myself that I will meditate later, just not now. The ritual you develop as you work through chapter 5 will help you avoid rationalizing delay. If you just take that first step in your ritual you will find it eases your way into sitting.

Falling asleep is a very common experience, especially for beginning meditators. It is important to recognize that you probably carry a buildup of stress, fatigue and exhaustion from having no time for yourself. Many meditation teachers believe that falling asleep is a form of resistance. I disagree with this interpretation. I believe it is most often due to long-term exhaustion. When you meditate in the morning this problem is minimized, but when it does happen it is a sign that your body and brain need rest. In early practice you will be discharging cumulative stress stored in the brain and body.

That said, falling asleep is something many people do when they feel emotionally overwhelmed. If it happens this way for you it can be thought of as a form of resistance, and you will benefit by asking yourself if you are flooded with feelings. Whatever the cause, it is a common symptom that usually disappears after the first few months.

It is very important to treat yourself gently when you miss your practice for a day or so. As I worked toward sitting regularly, I found that scolding myself made it more difficult for me to start again the next day. When I blamed myself it was because I felt guilty, which made me want to avoid sitting. Self-scolding will only make you more avoidant toward your meditation practice or any other regular discipline you are choosing to undertake.

Nobody Tells Me What To Do

Resistance has many positive functions. The power to control our own choices is something we learn in very early childhood, and it is deeply embedded in the psyche. We all learn to say no at about the age of two, long before we learn to say yes. It is healthy and adaptive, and asserts our separateness and right to self-determination. The power of no is the earliest way that children express their will, and consequently it is central to basic identity. (Stern, 2005) It occurs universally throughout the world at about the same age.

Unfortunately, parents often have difficulty dealing with the child's vocal claim to independence. This time in childhood is called the "terrible twos" for a reason. Too often children get locked in a power struggle with mother and father that can go on for years. Toilet training is an arena that is often the center of the battle, since it happens at about this same age. Parents who try to over-control the child are tempted to make her sit on the toilet too long. Of course the child rebels by refusing to cooperate, and mother is infuriated. In the final analysis, only the child can learn to control her own bodily functions, so the "no" position inevitably wins out. When the frustrated parent gives up on toilet training the power struggle generalizes to other arenas.

Too often the battle continues to rage through the growing-up years. The child is pushed into a corner and stubbornly hangs on to refusal. "No" becomes the automatic response, the only way the child/adolescent can maintain a sense of self. When we get stuck in this trap it is impossible to say yes. The automatic no becomes a default response to any suggestion, no matter how beneficial it is.

Nobody likes being told what to do, but some of us are permanently stuck in opposition and suffer the consequences. The child grows to adulthood balking at any rules or requirements, automatically refusing requests or advice. And sadly, we can't even do what we ourselves want. We can't take prescribed medications, and we're unable to meet the deadline for filing tax returns. "Nobody tells me what to do" means even I can't tell me what to do. In the service of becoming a person we sacrifice our freedom to say yes.

Meditation practice is a good example of this last dynamic. Sitting still for ten to fifteen minutes and counting your breaths each morning is a simple instruction. Yet resistance so often comes up. In training groups I have experienced many forms of "Nobody tells me what to do." People want to meditate lying down, they want to do it at night, and they would rather have a mantra or an imagery exercise, anything but just sitting still and counting their breaths.

Most of us have the problem of the automatic no to some degree, but it doesn't need to be crippling. Admit it to yourself and it loses most of its power to control your life. When you bring it to consciousness you free yourself to have a choice.

Now it is possible for you to choose yes. The automatic no is just like any interruption you experience in meditation. Under it is some feeling or memory that gives it energy. Many of us can recall the toilet training struggle. A client told me that her mother locked her in the bathroom until she produced a bowel movement. She learned to hold on and became chronically constipated: a lifelong burden.

You can restore your freedom. Reclaim the choice to say yes, when saying yes is what's best for you. Stop and think when the automatic no arises. Acknowledge your knee-jerk response to any request. Now you can freely consider your answer. Ask yourself what you really want to do and what is important to you, regardless of what others may advise. You actually do want the benefits of a regular meditation practice or you wouldn't be reading this book, and you want meditation even if we say it is good for you.

In our culture taking care of oneself is often considered self-ish and even narcissistic. However, your most primary respon-sibility is to take care of yourself. How can you have anything to give others if you don't take care of you? Self-care requires deciding you are worth that care. This neglectful attitude can be rooted in a deep sense of worthlessness. Feeling undeserv-ing or unworthy points to a wound inside that needs healing. Where did this unworthiness come from? When was the first time you felt it? You are carrying emotional pain that needs your loving attention.

We too often give priority to taking care of others, doing our jobs and going through the motions of life. Taking care of others is commendable except when you do it at your own expense. We call this co-dependency. It is a defense that helps you avoid your own feelings/issues. Used this way it is a form of self-abandonment. Co-dependency is a dangerous addictive disorder that ultimately leads to illness, disease and death. This is far too common. An example of this is the martyr wife who takes care of the alcoholic or addicted husband, wearing herself out and sacrificing her health. Underneath, she is afraid to set a boundary and say no. She is afraid of having to leave and be alone. Co-dependency is insidious and pervasive, and few people recognize its destructive power. It is just as powerful as alcoholism or drug addiction.

Don't nag and beat up on yourself when you miss a day of meditation. Instead try loving yourself into starting again today. Remind yourself that NWM, like regular exercise, is a gift you give yourself. It is not some punishment that you are forced to endure. This is one of my favorite ways of overcoming resistance. It is effective with any self-care habit that you are trying to build. I have noticed that it helps me keep up with regular exercise.

The Resistance is the Meditation

Resistance has its own body feeling. Experiment with letting yourself feel the impulse to resist in your body, whatever form it takes. For instance, you might experience restlessness. You have the impulse to get up and move around, do chores or make phone calls instead of meditating. Try sitting with the impulse but not responding. Now you have the opportunity to sense the full intensity of whatever feeling drives it. Trace the feeling to its source in your body. Then sit with it until it comes clear to you. Even the most uncomfortable feelings will ease up when given sufficient attention. Feeling the impulse to move but not responding builds your strength and your capacity for containment: the ability to hold in awareness even the most difficult feelings. This strength will serve you well in the transformational stage of healing that lies ahead.

With the discipline of containing the impulse the resistance itself becomes the meditation. Just relax and witness the impulse that drives your resistance, allow it to be just as it is, and be gently curious about it. Even though the resistance may be irritating, there must be something about it that works for you, or you wouldn't have it. When you enquire about it in this non-defensive way you open to new insight.

It helps to reflect upon the feeling quality of your resistance itself. Why do you choose this particular form of resistance? What is it about this pattern that feels right for you? Is this a way of avoidance you learned because it worked for you as a child?

You can make resistance your ally rather than your adversary. Everything about it is fuel for self-reflection: when and how it comes up, what form it takes and the feelings that go with it. Your path in NWM is one of expanding understanding, awareness and healing. Getting acquainted with your resistance is part of the journey.

Eight

Advancing Skills in Self-Enquiry

Daily practice is designed to peel away illusion and distortion, a process of gradually gaining insight. Over the months and years you realize more of your personal truth, one piece at a time. Inner peace and self-acceptance come through reconnecting to your personal truth, and to your authentic self. Only when you base life choices upon a solid connection to your true self can you live easily, harmoniously and joyfully

Making Friends with Anxiety

Working with resistance and anxiety is the way we begin to understand personal reality. Anxiety emerges as soon as you are able to overcome initial resistance. We harness the power of anxiety and make it our ally. The discomfort of anxiety points the way to secrets we have kept even from ourselves. Anxiety, like resistance, shows the way to something within you that wants to be known. We disarm anxiety and relax when we recognize it for what it is and then acknowledge and accept the truth of whatever is driving it. You will discover that anxiety is instantly disarmed once you discern its underlying cause.

Anxiety is a healthy survival mechanism and a normal part of emotional life. It is the uneasy feeling that comes when we think something bad is about to happen. It is the anticipation of fear rather than fear itself. Anxiety causes arousal of the sympathetic nervous system: an increased heart rate, shallow breathing, sweaty palms and often a tight and uneasy feeling in the stomach. When we feel threatened, adrenaline is released into the bloodstream along with cortisol, a stress hormone. The body is preparing for fight or flight. Worrying that a car might hit you as you leave the office is an experience of anxiety. In contrast, fear comes when we perceive an immediate threat. Imagine you are in the middle of the street and suddenly you see a speeding truck coming at you. This is fear. Anxiety creates the same physiological response as fear itself, but at a reduced level.

Change and uncertainty are the inherent nature of our existence. We don't know what the next moment may bring. This not knowing is an existential reality. We cannot eliminate uncertainty, but we can mitigate its effects. You can look both ways before you cross the street, buy new tires for your car, wear seatbelts, and have regular checkups. But uncertainty remains a reality that we must all learn to live with.

On the positive side, anxiety is very useful in dealing with the tests we so often face. When you have an appointment for a job interview it is normal to be anxious, and moderate anxiety works in your favor, increasing your ability to concentrate and sustain attention. This is also true for test taking. A certain amount of anxiety will actually increase your test score. On the other hand, when your anxiety level is too high it interferes with concentration and attention, reducing your ability to perform in the interview or on the exam.

Anxiety is your inner self calling for your attention; ignore it at your peril. It is a trouble signal, possibly a warning that something going on in your life is not right for you. The more intense the anxiety, the more important and urgent is the message. Of course your first impulse is to get rid of it as quickly as you can. We are so often tempted to cover our anxiety with external activities. But ignoring it is self-defeating, because it deprives you of the opportunity for discovery. As long as you are ignorant of its source you are flying blind, making decisions without full information. Even though anxiety makes you uncomfortable you don't need to run away. You will learn to use your anxiety as the powerful healing tool that it actually is. With experience you will be able to meet it with open and gentle curiosity, which allows it to reveal its source.

Anxiety is a common experience. It normally subsides when you solve the problem. Chronic anxiety, on the other hand, takes a long term toll on the body. It causes a continuous release of stress hormones into the blood stream and over years it is very detrimental to your health. It is important to your health, both mental and physical, to discover the cause and work it through.

Chronic anxiety can come from many sources, most commonly the events or circumstances of childhood. By the word circumstances, I mean the situation in which you find yourself, the uncontrollable facts of the world and family you were born into. You may not be aware that you have it until you are practicing regularly. Often it is like the paint on the wall. It is always there so we don't notice it until we get quiet inside. In meditation you meet and set aside the stuff of everyday anxiety. As you clear the space any underlying anxiety comes into awareness. Once you are aware of it you can sit with it and explore its source and relieve the stress that endangers your health. This is a wonderful benefit.

Getting to the source of your anxiety is a process of making conscious what was unconscious. This is the path of self-reflection, the path of healing: exploring the workings of your mind, bringing your history and your operating system into the light, getting to know how and why you make decisions and what you base those decisions upon.

The Nature of Healing

What we call healing is the step-by-step process of encountering and acknowledging your feelings, exploring their source, and finally coming to acceptance and self-forgiveness. All these stages are included in what we refer to as "working through" whatever comes up in meditation. This process, when complete, relieves the residual pain of past events.

In the musings and insights of everyday practice we sometimes experience emotional pain. It manifests in a body experience, quite often a marked tightness in the belly or chest. Pain is the body voice actively calling for your attention. Here is something that needs healing. It is actually a positive sign, because you have a constructive way of responding. The intensity of unease it carries is directly proportional to its healing potential. The more intense the discomfort, the greater the relief will be when you get the message the feeling is trying to convey.

Self-enquiry is a process of first noticing and then questioning. It begins when you notice a feeling of unease. Adopting an attitude of open and neutral curiosity is our way of inviting it to speak. First spend a few moments simply checking out the feeling, the sensation itself. You might ask the feeling what it is in your life that is bringing this up. Sit with both the sensation and the question. Most often words or images emerge to let you know what this might be about. Simply stay with the feeling to see what might come.

Anxiety guards the door to your inner truth. The message that awaits you hides inside. It is the truth of what you think or feel. Its meaning will be revealed when you can stay with the anxious feeling without judging, in the gently curious way of NWM. Allow yourself to hear the message simply as a matter of fact. For instance, maybe you realize there is a problem in an important relationship in your life, or you wake up to the impact of a childhood injury. When you know the truth, no matter what it is, you will feel relieved, even if it is not what you wished. Once revealed, it will seem obvious, because it is something you already knew. The truth has been there inside, waiting for you all along.

You will discover many layers of meaning. The first layer may be some superficial event of the day that leaves you with a sense of unease. Then you may recollect a moment of similar, more powerful anxiety from the past, even from childhood. Now you see this past event in a new way. Now you see how it has been shaping your view of life and your reactions, even after many years.

Remember that whatever it is may simply fade out of awareness at any point in this process. This is a normal and common experience. Resistance may be reasserting itself. If this is the case you can rest assured that the feeling will return at some point in the future, perhaps even later in this morning's practice. It is also possible that the feeling has conveyed all it needs you to know, at least for now. You are clearing your mind, which brings a feeling of relaxation. Simply return attention to the breath and continue sitting.

Things we go through, whether the sufferings or blessings of life, successes or failures, form lenses through which we view the world and ourselves. These lenses shape and even distort our perceptions and ways of thinking. They can lead to misinterpretation of now unfolding events. Not understanding the meanings we attach to past events prevents us from seeing things as they really are. The result of our misperceptions and misinterpretations is false expectations and misguided decision-making, disappointment and failure, pain and suffering. This is why emotional healing is so important.

The Felt-Certainty of Personal Truth

Your body recognizes each piece of your truth when you feel the connection between body sensation and its meaning. The meaning comes in words or images that correctly symbolize the body sense. This crucial connection completes the circuit. This is the body experience of insight. Recognition brings a sense of rightness in the body, a definite change inside, a sort of gut knowing that will make perfect sense. Then come relief and release.

The pieces of personal truth, once recognized, create permanent change. When we are called upon to make decisions we automatically fall back on our internal compass, this sense of rightness inside. This is the felt-certainty of your own personal truth. The path of healing is growing understanding of your personal reality. With time you find you are guiding your life from a strong whole sense of yourself that is new, different and more comfortable. The pieces have joined together to form a continuous interconnected network; a secure, body-based sense of your authentic truth.

The experience of insight is vivid, powerful and tremendously rewarding. You can see beyond the effects of the injuries and blessings of the past. It is not that you ignore past events. You will still honor their meaning and importance, but your new view of reality is vastly more comprehensive. Now you can live with growing personal authenticity.

Being connected to personal reality gives us something solid to stand upon, like the difference between standing on rock and standing on sand. It is a new sense of security. This feels so much better, so much more natural that you smoothly slide into living it. It fits like custom-made clothes. You feel no discontinuity; the old way simply fades away and is gone! You feel more secure in your choices, safer in guiding your life, because you have a solid congruence between your bodily-carried knowing and the choices you make along the way of life. This is the Body/Mind Wisdom at work.

Our personal reality is amazingly unique, complex and multilayered. It is dynamic, always changing as we take in and process new experience. It is a continuous unfolding of moment-to-moment living, reflected upon and integrated and then acted upon, creating yet another moment to be experienced.

The journey of healing always returns home to you—to living in and from your authentic self.

PART THREE:

TRANSFORMATIONAL HEALING

Nine

What Needs Healing

It turns out that we all need emotional healing because there is no such thing as perfect parenting. In addition, the circumstances of life are always problematic in one way or another. We all have feelings and memories going back to the very earliest days of childhood. We all carry a load of ignored, unrecalled and unexamined painful events from the past. They are our personal burden of emotional and physiological stress. Some of this trove of information doesn't require healing, it needs only to be understood, especially the ways it shapes our adult decisions and choices. Other pieces are wounds that require a deep process of healing: acknowledging the injury, grieving and coming to forgiveness.

Injuries and trauma we experienced in the past, especially in childhood, constitute a burden of suffering we have endured for years. It is hard to conceive of how profoundly this affects us. We are so used to suffering that we don't know it exists. We think of this burden as a normal part of life. It is as though we all wear a pair of glasses with lenses that are stained by our prior experiences, most importantly the pain of past injuries. We see everything through these lenses and so we are blind to the distortion they cause. In addition to making us unhappy, the burden of unhealed pain clouds our judgment, warps our decision-making and drains our energy. It even affects our physical health. Stress weakens the immune system, making us more vulnerable to all illness and disease.

Here we will explore what it is we are carrying that needs healing. We won't be talking about the things that go well, that increase our resilience and strength, but only those events that hurt. In the interest of preparation, remember that there is no absolute truth, only the truth of your own personal experience. All your feelings are valid. There is a real reason why you feel the way you do, even if you don't like it or don't even remember where it came from. The negative feelings we all carry inside are not easy to tolerate or accept, but they are part of our reality. Fear, anger, hatred, disgust, repulsion, jealousy, sadness and grief are the most difficult to accept, but they are the same as any other feeling, simply a natural part of being human. As you read along, notice what you feel in your body. Your body will signal recognition of the things we talk about here that ring true for you. They still live in your body memory.

Our emotional pain comes from three sources: the unavoidable circumstances of life, the trauma of childhood injury and the painful experiences of adult life. The most difficult and traumatic memories are those that come from childhood; the earlier in life the injury, the greater and more lasting the impact.

First, we will discuss the events of life over which we have no control. They begin with the inescapable accidents of birth, such as your race and gender and your physical characteristics. Even birth order has been found to have a very important impact on personality. All of the circumstances of our lives shape our experience and create unique situations we must navigate. They are the subject of many books. Here we can only touch on the effects of a few of these issues. We use these few examples so that you can get a feel for the broad range of different possibilities and the power of the effects of particular life situations.

The family you were born into is the single most important factor shaping your perceptions of life and the reality you must deal with. We can't help believing that our family is like every other family. We have nothing else to go on. But the truth is that every family is a unique ecosystem and has its own balance. The personalities and the psychodynamics of the family are stable or unstable, peaceful or violent, loving, harmonizing and cooperative or filled with conflict.

Each of us is born into a unique family which is our total experience in early life, and only gradually do we come out into the external world, as we start and continue school, make friends and grow to adulthood. The composition of the family, with its personalities, weaknesses and strengths, is the milieu in which we are immersed. Like swimming in the sea, we are completely absorbed in the family dynamic, subject to the waves, tides, storms and currents that surround us. Our parents had their own childhood experiences and found their own way. Their problems, hang-ups, happiness or depression, their injuries and traumas, successes, failures, all of who they are is our world, and we must cope with it, whatever issues it presents. They convey this to us verbally and nonverbally, in ways that are clearly observable and in ways so subtle we don't even notice what is happening. We take on their perceptions of reality. This is the only reality we know.

Hopefully your mother was sensitive to your reactions and needs. In psychology we call this wonderful harmonizing "empathic attunement." When this attunement works, you grow with an inner sense of well-being, peace and comfort. But sometimes things don't work so smoothly between the two of you. Mother has her own temperament and her own needs. If empathic attunement is missing, you will feel uncomfortable in the relationship.

I have seen videos of mother and baby where the baby is turning away from a mother who wants more interaction than her baby is comfortable with. The same baby is seen again as a child of six, having trouble tolerating close connection with mother and siblings, and even with other children at school. Of course, the situation can be reversed, with mother being aloof and distant while the baby wants and needs more contact. The images are very vivid, showing how strongly a mismatch affects the child's development.

What a powerful influence these first few months have on our lives. I was born during a time of war. My father deployed when I was three months old. Not only did I miss bonding with him, my mother was very frightened, preoccupied with worry about my father's safety. Because of her fear mother was not fully available for me. My mother's anxiety transferred to me even as a baby. I carry a fear of abandonment that I'm sure will always be with me. I believe my mother's anxiety became hard-wired into my nervous system because of the very early nature of the experience. This underlying anxiety is what first led me to begin meditation.

You might have abandonment anxiety if your mother became ill early in your life and needed to go to the hospital, or if a parent passed away during your childhood, or even if your mother or father was emotionally distant and cool, rather than warm and loving, or emotionally unavailable for whatever reason. On the other hand, if your mother was too close, over-bearing and smothering, making demands upon you for companionship she should have received from other adults, you may need space and have trouble being close.

We all have a unique story to tell. Maybe you grew up during the Cold War, when everyone was afraid. Maybe the family you were born into happened to be wealthy, or was very poor. Maybe your parents fought constantly and finally divorced, or stayed together in spite of a conflicted relationship. Maybe you were lucky, and your parents had a loving and supportive marriage.

Parenting style is intergenerational in nature. Events in our parents' lives, especially their own childhood experiences, affect how they treat us. We all come to adulthood with distinct ways of viewing the world, shaped by our own past as well as those of the thousands of generations preceding us. Thus the effects of childhood are passed down unconsciously from generation to generation. Something that happened to your great-great-grandmother can still be affecting you today, determining your responses to people and situations you now encounter.

The all-too-common tendency to abuse and neglect children is also passed down from prior generations. (Miller, 1983, 2006) No matter how many books we read about best ways of parenting, when our children are out of control we tend to respond the same way our parents did. So the history of abusive patterns goes back over thousands of generations.

We are trained to be grateful to our parents for all that they have given us. This is a Biblical and also Confucian imperative that many of us have internalized. I have heard so many people excuse their parent's behavior, rationalizing that the punishment they received was well deserved, or it was normal and everybody did it.

When we deny the reality of what happened it can never be healed. It remains untouched inside, ready to come out when we have children of our own. When we pretend to ourselves that it was somehow okay that we were abused, we will blindly repeat the pattern with our own children. Then our children are likely to abuse their children. This is the terrible legacy of child abuse.

The only way to stop the intergenerational legacy of abuse is to bring your memories to consciousness. Some people have clear memories of abusive events in childhood; other abuse victims remember nothing. In NWM you may spontaneously recall childhood abuse in your own life. Memories of childhood trauma do not come easily into awareness for two important reasons. First, they are stored in the midbrain and not readily available to consciousness. Secondly, we want to protect ourselves from recalling the terrible pain of the abuse itself: the shame, humiliation and betrayal we suffered at the hands of the people we loved and trusted the most. If we admit to ourselves the truth of what happened, we are forced to see our parents in a new light. As a result there is an automatic and unconscious layer of defenses protecting us from painful recollections.

Child neglect is a powerful source of crippling that continues all through life. If our parents don't take care of us, how can we possibly learn to take care of ourselves? We can't. So we grow up neglecting ourselves emotionally and even physically. Sometimes just providing adequate food is too much to handle. Just like abuse, neglect is passed down through the generations. If you were not held, cuddled and soothed as a small child you won't feel comfortable giving your child that love. It won't even occur to you that she needs it. In order to end the chain of neglect, you must be conscious of your own injury and go through a healing process, and you will still need to work toward good parenting every day.

A client, Robert, told me that when he was two years old his mother would go out and leave him alone to take care of his little sister, who was a baby at the time. He learned how to open a can of beans all by himself, so that he could feed his baby sister. His mother was quite proud of his accomplishments and independence. He had no way of knowing that this was not normal. As a result, he grew up to feel that he could and should handle everything himself. Because he couldn't rely on his mother he couldn't trust that anyone would be there to support him. He was unable to trust his wife or any family member to deal with problems successfully, so his relationship with his wife was stunted and distant. He was suffering from the terrible loneliness of not being able to trust.

Neglected children grow up with a feeling of isolation and loneliness that is pervasive and leaves a lifelong sense of emptiness and longing. They can never fill this longing in adult relationships, because it isn't about their mate, it is about the mother and father of long ago. They sometimes come to me for couple therapy struggling to get this need met.

The experience of abuse and neglect leaves a residue of shame. You feel that it was your fault, that something must be wrong with you, and that you are somehow bad or unworthy. Even when you have completely repressed the memories of abuse, the feeling of shame remains. The abused or neglected child hears a clear shaming message from parents, "You are bad. There is something wrong with you." Your father or mother is saying, "I don't love you, I don't want you. You are a worthless piece of garbage." The burden of these painful messages is internalized in the child's mind and heart, and is carried along to adulthood, making it impossible to have a happy and satisfying life. Victims often continue through life choosing relationships in which the abuse is repeated.

Physical abuse is widespread, far more common than most of us know. It leaves the child with a pervasive feeling of fear, always waiting for the next episode of screaming or punishment, the next beating. Sexual abuse is even more damaging to the development of the growing child. The message of the sexual abuser is so demeaning and humiliating. The abuser is saying "You are nothing. You exist only for my pleasure. Your needs and your safety count for nothing." The child feels totally used and irreparably betrayed.

Shame can come from more subtle devaluing attitudes conveyed by parents. It can begin early in childhood with something like mother's dirty look when she catches you masturbating. When parents are repelled by your natural human needs and functions they are sending a toxic message of shame about your very existence as a living being. Usually we grow up without awareness of the shame we carry. The shaming messages begin so early in life that we don't have verbal memories. But the body remembers and carries the bad feelings deep inside. They are incorporated into the operating system in the form of self-shaming and low self-esteem.

Even seemingly subtle failures of parenting have a lasting effect. A failure of empathy on the part of parents leaves a residue of suffering. Pain and disappointment in childhood often come from mother or father's inability to offer you even the most basic attunement, the feeling of being seen and heard, the deep connection we all need. Too many parents see their children merely as an extension of themselves, not as separate beings with unique needs and preferences. Babies and children are people too and they desperately long to be accurately seen and understood.

One day David and I were walking along our favorite path enjoying the view when along came a beautiful young couple with an adorable little boy who was about 18 months old, still unsteady on his feet. We stopped and said hi to the child, talking directly to him and smiling. He responded immediately with a big smile and began to try to talk to us in his limited language. After a few minutes we realized that the couple wanted to go on down the path, so we had to say goodbye. Even though it has been years since this event, we haven't forgotten what happened. The child turned around and reached out to us as we walked away, stretching out his little arms and crying to come with us, as though we were his long-lost family. Our short encounter with this little boy triggered his longing for love and connection. Children immediately recognize what they need when it is offered.

This couple was obviously affluent. I'm sure they were taking perfect care of their child in the material world, but they were not connecting with him. This is what happens when parents treat children as objects. The beautiful young couple probably had the same experience when they were children. And so the legacy of neglect and the failure of empathy continues to be passed on to succeeding generations.

Of course, not all childhood trauma is due to failures of parenting, child abuse or neglect. Accidents and illnesses in childhood can also leave traumatic memories with a lasting impact. Whatever the scars of childhood, we bring them all with us into adult life, most often blindly. Our blindness robs us of free choice; we are completely unaware of how the influences that shaped our upbringing now drive our responses to the events of life.

Issues of Adult Life

There are so many challenges we all face in adult life. Some of them are tests we create for ourselves. Because of our childhood injuries we make errors in judgment, leading to painful mistakes and missed opportunities. We find ourselves facing very difficult choices, and challenges that may seem impossible to overcome. Even though they hurt, these errors in judgment put pressure on us to look deeply inside and ask why. What was behind this choice? This forces intense introspection that can be very fruitful. To me, as an outside observer or even considering issues in my own life, many of these dilemmas seem almost diabolical in their perfection. They are perfect in their design. We must look inside and face the truth, take the path of growth and health, or remain forever stuck in repeated destructive patterns.

Some of the trauma we experience in adult life comes out of the blue, completely outside of our control. We each have our own list of the most difficult and traumatic events of our lives, but there is some research on this topic we can use to direct us toward what are the most common and most serious traumatic events we may face.

This research was first attempted by Holmes and Rahe in a study published in 1967. The researchers wanted to know if life stress caused illness, and if so, which events were the most serious predictors. They studied the medical records of 5,000 patients. They gave them a list of stressors and asked them which of these had occurred in their lives in the prior twelve months. In a later study they followed 5000 sailors over time, to see how many visits they made to the hospital and whether they were forced to drop out of any special training due to illness. From these findings the researchers rated the relative impact of their list of stressors. Holmes and Rahe came up with a list of 43 major stressful events. Here are the top ten most stressful events in adult life, based on their findings:

Death of a spouse
Divorce

Marriage separation
Jail term
Death of a close relative
Injury or illness
Marriage
Fired from job
Marriage reconciliation
Retirement

These research findings were validated in a number of subsequent studies by different research teams working with different populations. All of these circumstances are reasons why people become depressed, angry and anxious, and ultimately get physically sick. Not mentioned in this list are natural disasters such as severe storms, earthquakes, hurricanes, floods, or losing your home in a fire. These are all tests of our ability to cope in the face of adversity and recover from loss.

Let us not forget that on top of all the possible trauma we face, each of us comes to adulthood with a fully-developed operating system; we carry an invisible suitcase full of ideas, beliefs, attitudes and feelings along with a collection of memories from our childhood experience. This baggage shapes our responses to the hurdles we face, making these major stressors easier or more difficult for us to overcome, in complex ways that we are most often not aware of.

Freud said that we can't be happy unless we are functioning well in both work and love. Every hurdle we face in adult life will be more or less difficult for us depending upon how it was for us as children. It is not uncommon for someone to do extremely well at work, and build a great career, while having terrible difficulties in finding a mate, forming a family and having children. Some people have great difficulty both in work and in love.

Very few of us have an easy time. When we face a challenge that is particularly difficult it can provoke a crisis, with intense emotional pain. Such crises are turning points in life where we can either move ahead or remain stuck.

Every loss recapitulates all our prior losses. If your mother died when you were a child, losing an aunt or dear friend when you are in your thirties may bring intense grief, coming as a reminder of your earlier wound. In this way events piggyback on each other. New traumas echo the trauma of the past, magnifying the intensity of your feelings.

One young man I knew had major surgery as a small child. Later on, as a teen, he was injured in a skate board accident. He needed surgery as a result of the accident, but was repelled by the idea of being anesthetized. He carried an unconscious memory of his very early surgery that left him filled with fear. He was lucky to find a psychologist who would hypnotize him, and he was able to undergo the surgery without pain.

When trauma occurs very early in life we have no conscious memory, but its impact lingers on, magnifying our responses to current events. You can tell that a prior event is intensifying your feelings by the level of pain that is evoked by the current event. I have learned to watch for this when it happens to clients and students who are triggered by current events that are not important enough in themselves to account for the level of emotional response. When you find yourself unusually upset about something, ask inside if this in any way reminds you of a childhood event. Often simply recognizing the link calms the current upset. Here is another opportunity for insight and growth.

Relationships

Choosing a mate and creating a healthy and stable relationship is a challenge for many people. If your parents were happy together, if you were planned and wanted and given lots of love in childhood, if your parents had a stable healthy relationship, it will be easier for you to find an appropriate mate and start a family. Deep in your psyche you carry an image of a happy, healthy couple. You carry a sense inside of what it means, what it is, and how to be part of such a couple, and so it is natural for you to choose a mate, build a strong relationship and eventually have a family.

On the other hand, it might be that you can't ever find a mate. It might be that you choose inappropriate people, with whom you can't succeed. Some people go from one relationship to the next, unable to make a commitment. Others get into negative and even destructive relationships, repeating the injuries of childhood and suffering the same kind of emotional pain over and over.

If you have your needs met in babyhood, you grow up being capable of trust and therefore of intimacy. If the attunement is missing in infancy, you grow up having a hard time trusting, which makes it difficult to form a lasting close relationship. If mother is too close, making you feel smothered, you will have trouble being intimate as you grow older. In spite of your natural longing for love, closeness will bring inner conflict, a sense of tension and unease. If mother was too distant and cool, you will grow up longing for closeness.

It seems we are mysteriously compelled to re-create our family of origin, and select people who make us feel the same way our parents did. It really isn't such a mystery after all, when you consider that we can only create what we know. How could we possibly be drawn to an emotionally healthy person and build a strong family when we have no healthy model? Freud recognized this dynamic in what he called the repetition compulsion, an unconscious attempt to heal the wound of the past. Somehow we believe that if we can just love this neglectful or abusive person enough, they will change their ways and become the loving partner we long for. "If I am a good enough boy or girl, mommy will love me" turns into a dream that I can be a good enough lover or partner so that my mate will change into the loving partner I long for, and then my wound will be healed. This is a dream of healing that never works.

This dynamic was very active in my own life. Because of my abandonment anxiety I was repeatedly attracted to unavailable men. My first marriage was to a mathematician who was extremely withdrawn and alcoholic. Looking back, I know that I had a dream. He was good-looking, brilliant, well-educated and had a good job. I saw my prince in him. Through my love I would help him to open up so that he could be present for me. But of course it didn't work, and over the years I grew terribly lonely. I loved him very much. We met when we were very young and had a lot in common. As the relationship disintegrated I felt as though my life was at stake. I was becoming depressed. After a long struggle I was able to leave the marriage. In the weeks right after I left I felt a deep wound in my chest, as though I had been cut open and was bleeding. It was the loss of a dream, rather than loss of the actual relationship, that caused me the most suffering.

In recovery from the divorce, and from my childhood injury, I dated a number of men. I was intent on understanding relationships and how they worked or didn't work for me, and why. Finally through my meditation practice and psychotherapy I was able to heal the wound. The amazing part was that the kind of men I was attracted to changed completely. I found that as soon as a man indicated in any way that he was afraid of connecting, distant or avoidant of his feelings, I was turned off and would drop the relationship. Finally I met David, a completely different kind of person, open to intimate connection and honest about his feelings.

There is no quick fix for changing the kind of person we are drawn to. Remember that the neural patterns that define what we think of as love are formed in the very earliest months and years of life. The memories that built this pattern are preverbal and not available to conscious thought. Our bodies remember the feeling, the smells and the tone of voice, the skin texture of mother and father, and so we are drawn to people who smell, sound, and feel "right."

Change is not impossible. Before NWM these patterns could be changed only through long-term psychotherapy. Now, daily meditation practice over years connects you to the Body/Mind Wisdom, the bodily-carried memories. You will be learning how to do this in the coming chapters.

Having Children and Parenting

When it comes to building a family, there are so many ways things can go well or badly. There are issues of fertility/infertility, which can be very difficult. I have worked with couples who were suffering because they couldn't have children. Struggling with infertility can be such severe stress that it causes a breakup, especially when people get married with the intention of having a family.

Having a child is very stressful. There are many hazards in pregnancy and birth. These are life-threatening times for both mother and child. Even children who are wanted and planned bring stress, especially in the first two years of life, when they need constant attention and caring. Children bring great joy at the same time that they make big demands. They are a huge responsibility, and raising them properly takes a major part of our energies through all our adult lives. Some people find it very frightening to love another human being as much as we love our children. Loving brings such vulnerability. Fear of loving reflects an early wound that needs to be understood and healed.

One of the most painful blows we can sustain is giving birth to a child with a birth defect, retardation or autism. Parents who have defective children tend to blame themselves even when blame is completely unwarranted. This is very emotionally devastating, leaving a lasting wound. Even though the parents may make an adjustment and cope well with what happened, there will always be a painful place inside. The worst part of this is realizing that there is nothing we can do to make it better for the child we love so much.

Having a child that you cannot support and giving that child up for adoption leaves a painful mark that never goes away. Abortion leaves a painful scar on the mother and very often on the father as well. It hurts, even when we know we can't be good parents to the child. Women who have abortions pay a high price. The body bonds to the embryo even in the very first few weeks after conception, so the loss is great. The impact of abortion on the father has been vastly underestimated. In clinical practice I find that fathers of babies who are aborted feel a great sense of loss, and they grieve as much as the women do. Couples who stayed together after an abortion often get caught up in blaming each other for the loss of the child.

Parenting continues, in different forms, even after children leave home and are living on their own. All through our lives we will be concerned about how our children are doing in their own work and relationships and with our grandchildren. We will always be vulnerable to being hurt by anything bad that happens in their lives. If this is the price of parenting, then the rewards are equally huge. First we get the joy of watching them grow up and become self-governing individuals. We feel pride in their successes and accomplishments. We get to know them as the unique individuals they are, and this is a tremendous pleasure in itself. When they grow up they bring their wives and husbands into the family, and eventually their children. Grandchildren are especially rewarding. There is a profound satisfaction and joy in knowing that the family lives on even after we die.

Issues of Work, Career and Money

Your station in life, in most countries, is determined by the wealth and success of your parents. Upward mobility, as defined by rising above the income quintile into which you were born, is the exception, rather than the rule. Having parents with successful careers gives you the idea that you too can be successful. With this expectation embedded in your operating system, you do your best at the good schools provided by your affluent parents. You leave school well prepared and step right into a good job. I've seen this happen, but I have also seen exceptions. Each family is unique, with its own dynamics.

Of course the opposite could be true. You could be born into a family where your father and mother were not successful at making a good living for whatever reason. What they conveyed to you was not the attitudes and feelings of successful people, who take for granted that you will be successful too.

On the contrary, their message was that life is difficult; poverty is always a threat or even a reality. Instead of conveying self-confidence, they express their own fears, which we as children take in. Their negative attitudes are a handicap we carry with us. Then if we don't get the education we really need it's very difficult for us to succeed.

I find it fascinating the way people choose jobs that somehow reflect their childhood experience. A particular teacher who is inspiring can shape your choice of career. It is more common to follow in the footsteps of your father or mother. Sometimes people choose a career designed to heal a wound of the past. If you were a neglected or abused child you may choose to be in the helping professions where you can prevent these injuries from happening to the children or families in your care. If your mother or father was ill for years during your childhood you may decide to become a physician or a nurse.

No matter what job you choose you will be affected by the society around you. Our capitalist system is plagued with cycles of boom and bust, recessions and times of prosperity. These cycles can have profound effects on your job and your income. You can be laid off or fired in a time of recession and have difficulty getting another job at a very formative time in your career, resulting in a long-term reduction of your earnings. Starting your own business creates its own stresses. Instead of working from 9 to 5 you work from 5 to 9, which takes a toll on body and mind, and burdens your personal life, your marriage and your children.

There is so much each of us needs to heal. We want to impress you with the sheer number and seriousness of the issues all of us face, to get you thinking deeply about your own life, and how your path is shaped by your past. We invite you to consider your childhood and the issues you are dealing with now, whether in work or in love. What needs healing in you?

Personally, I found writing this chapter to be a difficult experience. For years I have heard the stories of clients and students, and accompanied them on the path of healing. As I wrote I recalled many of their stories and felt for the suffering I've witnessed. I did not include any of the many true stories of real abuse. I left them out to protect you from the vicarious trauma you might suffer from reading them. I hope that this chapter will help you to feel for your own suffering, to begin to acknowledge all you carry within you that needs healing.

David and I are excited about the deep and profound healing process we will be teaching in the coming chapters. We know the truth of this process from our own experience as well as from clients and students I have worked with. Optimal health, both physical and mental, is within your reach, even though that may be hard for you to believe right now. The rewards of healing are beyond what you can imagine. They are the comfort and sense of security you long for, the self-acceptance and self-love that will make you whole, and the immense reward of living to your full creative potential.

Ten

In The Crucible

In the Bronze Age, more than 5000 years ago, human beings discovered how to extract metal from ore by placing it in a crucible, a container made from fireproof ceramic. When heat was applied, the ore melted to release the molten metal. This primitive smelting evolved into what we now know as the science of metallurgy.

Alchemy is the mythical medieval practice of transforming lead into gold. The Alchemists thought of lead as the most impure metal, while they saw gold as the most refined. In the process of transformation, catalyzed by the mystical Philosopher's Stone, the lead would melt in the heated crucible to release the molten gold.

Carl Jung used the term Alchemy as a metaphor for healing and transformation in psychotherapy. Jung's Alchemy is the distillation of the fully conscious Self, the gold, from the raw material of the unconscious undifferentiated personality, the lead. He distinguished between the raw undeveloped self (small s) – the *prima materia* – and the transformed fully-developed Self (uppercase S). In analysis, the crucible is the safe and secure container of the therapeutic relationship. The heat that is applied is the honest encounter with the analyst.

The strength of your commitment to daily practice is your crucible of transformation. No matter how intense your feelings become, you continue to sit in meditation every day. You yourself are the magical Philosopher's Stone. The fire of sustained daily practice directly ignites the transformational process by which the *prima materia* is heated and finally melts. Your transformed and fully-developed Self is forged in the crucible of daily practice.

Spiritual transformation is the natural culmination of the practice of New World Meditation. Awakening comes in a progressive flow of change, from beginning practice through an intermediate phase and into this advanced stage. The method is the same simple steps you learned in chapter 4, but the process is more intense in advanced practice. On this journey of transformation you will gradually but relentlessly penetrate to your true essence, getting clear on who you are and what is important to you. At the same time your consciousness expands, becoming more inclusive and growing your capacity for empathy for yourself and others.

From the beginning you are continually clearing out old painful experiences. By the time you reach advanced practice you have made peace with much of your old baggage. We do not deny the reality of what happened in the past, but these issues are no longer living inside you, causing pain and distorting your perceptions. Now, whatever remains that is challenging awaits the transformative stage of healing.

The change that lies ahead will bring self-forgiveness, the entry to compassion. It is the healing process itself that allows the inner essence to emerge. The unfolding of the infinite Self continues all through life, even after Awakening. It is never complete, always ongoing, forever in process. Our goal in this chapter is to describe the expanding and blossoming of the Self in daily practice. Along the way you will discover that you are stronger than you thought, more resourceful than you imagined, and far more courageous than you ever dreamed.

In the Heat

When you sit to meditate you look over your life, all of it, a little at a time. In the silence of meditation the heat of self-encounter melts through all pretenses, honesty breaks through and your truth emerges into the light of waiting awareness, revealing what happened in the past and showing you how it is still affecting you today. Important events are brought back to life by today's happenings, which echo unresolved events of the past. Each day is another check-in to how you feel now, what happened yesterday, how you felt and now feel about it, whatever is coming up today, your choices and their conse-quences, time and its passing. The continuing effects of old stories are unfinished business, which you will now complete.

Life hands us tests, and we create tests for ourselves: chal-lenges to be faced and problems to be solved. Sometimes we create crises that demand solutions. Each of these tests asks us to reach inside and find the way to choices that fit for us. You carry inside an essential knowing, the felt-certainty of your per-sonal truth. Now, in advanced practice, it calls more urgently for consciousness. Provoked by events, it comes freshly, perhaps in a flash of newly revealed meaning. As it comes to awareness you begin to count on this new meaning and rely on it to point the way to your truth. You set the pace of Awakening with the rhythm of your inner readiness.

The layers of your operating system, your mind and per-sonality, are revealed in their own order. We cannot pre-dict the flow of your personal progress. Sometimes material stored in the midbrain, memories of traumatic moments, will spontaneously emerge. You may suddenly recognize the ways they have shaped your operating system. You might even re-live an experience that was especially powerful, along with all its associated feelings and images.

You will be amazed at the many ways that old stories and trauma have determined the course of your life. At times new awareness will come as an unwelcome surprise. It is difficult to face the fact that you made mistakes and poor choices in the past. You hurt other people; at times you hurt yourself, by act-ing in a way that betrayed your true nature.

On the positive side, you will gain insight and new appre-ciation of the gifts you received from life's experiences, even the painful ones. At the time it may have been difficult, and you acknowledge this reality. But now you see a gift in that memory that has enriched your life. Many of the challenges gave you strength, and now they may bring you great enjoyment.

You will recognize things in you that you have always known but haven't acknowledged. The jolt of newly-revealed truth is only temporary. As you spend some time trying on new insight, multiple dimensions come to awareness. You will see with new eyes all the consequences and ramifications of what happened. Now you have options and you can make new choices.

One day in meditation I noticed a subtle underlying anxiety. As I sat with it for a few minutes I realized I was uneasy about having my husband's approval. Because I have been practicing for many years, I was quickly able to follow the thread of the feeling back in time. There I found the same uneasy feeling in my childhood: my relationship with an abusive father who was impossible to please. As a result I experienced difficulty in love relationships and spent years without a partner. Even though I worked on this issue in therapy, the residual pain lingered on.

In that moment I saw that my anxiety came from wishing for so long that my father would love me and approve of me. My longing for his love was part of my operating system. I was running my life on the assumption that I would never experience real acceptance and love.

The insight I gained that morning allowed me to acknowledge my suffering and open my heart to myself, as a child and as a woman. Because of my childhood experience it was hard for me to believe in the possibility of love and happiness. Now I carry this differently in my body. Now I have the felt-certainty inside. I know I am lovable. I know that David loves me and approves of me. I know that I am fine just the way I am. I have my own approval, my own acceptance and love, which is the most important.

The practice of NWM brings you home to your true Self. Change itself always carries fear of the unknown. Some people imagine they will be completely different, but these fears are unfounded. Your core self will not change. On the contrary, you will be more comfortable being who you truly are. You will discover that your life will be better, happier and more productive.

At last you have the chance to make peace with the past so that you can move on to living in the bliss of the now. No more carrying the burden of old baggage. Sometimes the changes we dream of seem so remote. It can be frightening to hope for a better life, because hope brings vulnerability. We so often carry a fixed idea that big changes are impossible, especially in dealing with the issues that hurt us most. It is time to let go of this old way and accept that change can happen, healing is possible and you can be relieved of even your oldest and most painful injuries.

The transition is like a near-death experience in the sense that it opens your consciousness to a whole new reality. The near-death experiences we hear about in the popular press happen in situations that are out of control: when the plane almost goes down, in a terrifying auto accident, or on the operating table. This is different. Here you are making a conscious choice to move ahead, on your own power, through healing and into Awakening.

The healing transition may evoke intense anxiety and fear. Fear surrounds and cloaks all the most terrible memories: of trauma or abuse, serious accidents or illnesses and the most difficult circumstances of life. It is fear of the truth of the memory.

In order to avoid the fear, we set up a complex system of protective defense mechanisms. The more suffering we have experienced, the more energy we invest in our defenses. They help us to forget what happened, or park it away in the back of the mind, or rationalize that it didn't hurt after all. Our defenses take many different forms, all of which serve the same purpose, the avoidance of our feelings. Our defense mechanisms are embedded into the operating system and they work automatically and unconsciously.

One of the most commonly used defenses is rationalization, an intellectual attempt to assemble reasons why whatever happened is fine after all. I speak openly to friends about child abuse. I believe it must be brought out into the light if it is ever going to be eliminated. It amazes me when friends who are intelligent and well-educated rationalize the abuse they suffered as a child by saying that they deserved it, or that everyone did it. This is their way of sheltering themselves from the pain of the truth: that the parent they loved abused them. Then they proceed to tell me that they have to hit their own children in order to teach them how to behave. And so the cycle of abuse continues on to the next generation.

Often when I bring up the issue, people get angry. What starts out as simple conversation turns into a heated argument. I have challenged their defenses and they don't want to face the truth. Staying safe is so important to them that they experience my words as a threat.

Defenses are automatically triggered to help us hold onto sanity in the face of overwhelming stress. Not all of our memories of trauma are conscious. The mind wants to protect us from traumatic memories that are too much for us to handle. Freud referred to this as repression. It is a very powerful defense because it causes us to completely and automatically forget any overwhelming event. It requires massive amounts of psychic energy, so we only use it for the most horrific intolerable memories. In advanced practice repressed memories can spontaneously return to consciousness. When repression lifts and reveals severe trauma, you may feel overwhelmed, and need to seek out a therapist to help you work through your feelings. In general, those memories won't return until you have built the necessary strength.

There are less powerful mechanisms that we use more often that also result in forgetting what happened. Suppression is making a conscious decision not to remember the event. Compartmentalization is unconsciously putting the event away in the back of your mind. In these mechanisms the memory is more available than in repression. When something comes up that reminds you of the event, the door opens, and you suddenly recover the whole memory of what happened. When reminded, you will recognize that you knew it all along; it was just hidden away in that closet.

Defenses protect you but they also box you in, limiting your world and possibilities. Through blocking awareness they prevent healing. In order to heal it is essential to see your defenses for what they are and validate the pain that caused you to build them. Yes, there was trauma, and yes, you were hurt. This was and continues to be your reality. It can never be healed and put aside until you admit it to yourself. This acknowledgement is the most basic and fundamental validation of your reality. You are re-owning your own reality and acknowledging your pain and suffering. Letting go of lying to yourself is a tremendous relief. Now you can feel empathy for you, as the child you were and the person you are today. This insight is the entry to compassion, opening your mind and heart to you, your story and your suffering.

Dealing With Fear

Fear is such a powerful negative that we automatically learn very quickly how to avoid it. Fear has a way of generalizing. This phenomenon is referred to in psychology as stimulus generalization.. Anything that happens at the same time as a fear-producing event will come to elicit the same reaction as the event itself. For example, if as a child you were in an accident while on a carnival ride, you may never feel comfortable going to a carnival again. Everything about it, the smell, the sounds, the lights and colors, can become fear-producing.

With time the generalizing expands so that any bright lights or loud noises begin to bring the same response. You may learn to fear the noise of crowds or loudspeakers, the smell of popcorn, even when they have nothing to do with a carnival. The ripple effects of trauma keep expanding so that there are more and more things to be afraid of. Your choices are narrowed as you build your life within the bounds set by your fears. Eventually you live in a very restricted world. If an accident on a carnival ride can result in this kind of fear, you can imagine the terrible effects of childhood trauma and especially abuse, whether emotional, physical or sexual.

Fear is especially challenging when there is nothing we can do in the external world to change the fear-provoking circumstance. All the biological manifestations of fear ultimately work to protect us from death. The fear of death is hard-wired into the brain. It can never be completely overcome, nor would we want to eliminate it.

As hard as it may be for you to believe, you can face and live through the fire of your fears. Here is the paradox: it turns out that going through the fear and touching into the softer underlying feelings is actually a way to the transformational healing you long for. Going through the fear brings you to self-empathy. You feel the sadness and grief that comes with recognizing your own suffering. What you feel is the longed-for self-love. Now comes the vision of yourself as you once were and still are, tender and vulnerable. At the core of grief is the limitless loving compassion that has been dormant deep in your heart. It is set free through this healing transition, flowing through and from your heart in a river of loving energy.

Along the path of NWM you experience many powerful feelings. You already know that feelings melt and change when they are fully attended to. Even fear loses its power over you when you face it directly. Fear, like all feelings, melts in the light of awareness. Your own nonjudgmental loving acknowledgment and full accepting attention is all that is needed to end your suffering.

Here's the rub: you must have great willingness and courage. It will take some moments for the truth to emerge. During this time you must sustain your presence with the fear itself. There is heat, but it doesn't burn. It is the heat of intense reality. The intensity of the fear will melt into ecstatic bliss when you move through it into the light of pure awareness.

This ultimate journey of deepest self-reflection is, by its nature, a revolution in consciousness. Facing your fears and all your feelings, even including the fear of illness, disease and death, is the spiritual transformation. Sitting with pure fear is amazing and life-changing. You will awake to the reality that there is nothing to fear after all.

Your body/mind has its own powerful healing energy, guided by the intuitive knowing you carry inside. In NWM you hook into the power of this healing energy. It is an amazing current of potential, activated by daily practice. You are always moving forward into health and expanding consciousness.

David and I don't have a map of your personal path, and we can't predict your pace. It is the same for all of us: we only experience the path as it unfolds, we can't see around the next bend until we get there. We are each on our own unique journey. Healing will come by seeing through your defenses to the pain they cover. Or it will come through facing your fears. It is the heart opening that is the key. When you can validate your own personal reality your heart will open to all that you are.

The Self is infinite, it is like a flower that continues to unfold and expand as long as you continue your journey of self-enquiry. Your habit of meditation is the same every day and it is very simple. All you need to do is sit quietly and go within. Yet the experience is always new and always fresh. On this lifetime path of exploring the infinite Self you will always be moving along toward greater awareness. Healing is beyond insight and growth; it is all that and more. It is the transition to Awakening.

Eleven

Advanced Practice

Our defenses are strong when it comes to memories of trauma, especially early trauma. They protect us from seeing and acknowledging things about ourselves and our families that we find unacceptable. We lie and hide the truth even from ourselves to avoid the pain and shame we carry inside.

All through your practice you face and work through your injuries. Some of your burden of suffering is already resolved and is in the past. Now, in advanced practice, you are down to the primary original wounds that still linger. They are at the very foundation of your operating system. This is why this core healing is such a profound shift, finally restoring you to wholeness and bringing you to Awakening.

Usually memories of early trauma surface only when your practice has matured. You may know the facts of what happened, but the emotional impact of the injury will most often remain hidden. Early injuries and the feelings they carry emerge in advanced practice. They come in insights we gain in deep moments of self-reflection. At first you may feel overwhelmed, but you do have the necessary strength to work through these issues. It is the strength you built and are continuing to build in the cauldron of daily practice. You will have experienced the process of healing many times along the way. You know from experience that the process is basically the same, no matter what injury you are dealing with.

There are three essential elements in healing: dropping judgment, allowing yourself to see the whole truth, and coming to self-forgiveness. These three processes do not lend themselves to any simple stepwise listing. They do not unfold in any linear fashion. No one of them can work by itself; each is intertwined with and dependent upon the others. Sometimes you see an event in your past that you had forgotten, and feel the pain of it for some time before you can drop judgment and forgive yourself. Sometimes the key elements of healing come all at once. In a sudden rush of insight you see an important piece of your past plainly, just as it was, and come to forgiveness in that same moment.

We heal in stages, determined by the body's own unique pace. As you release each layer of suffering, another one is revealed, and must be faced. If you avoid dealing with this next layer, it will keep coming up until you decide to pay attention and acknowledge it as your own. The body won't let go of the pain until healing is complete. In advanced practice you are connecting to core feelings, the earliest wounds and the most primary layers of your operating system.

Take a moment to recall the metaphor of the layers of an onion, which we evoked in chapter 3. Unlike the onion, the layers of your operating system are not separate. Your personal reality is constructed over time, each set of parameters building upon and modified by the ones before. They are integrated and fully interconnected, so that the process of gaining insight and coming to a new perspective is always complex.

By the time you reach advanced practice you will have a much greater understanding of the past events you have already worked through. You will see how some injuries affected your behavior and shaped your operating system. Each major insight re-frames your view of other past events. You see other pieces of your operating system in new light, pieces that you have encountered before and may have struggled with for years.

We know that words are not enough to describe the experience of deep healing. It can only be understood by living through it yourself. As we continue, we will consider the complex dilemmas faced in advanced practice. We want to show you how healing clears the way for your true nature to emerge. This way you will be ready to understand our description of the fully healed and whole human being we will present in the final chapter of this book.

Judging and Blaming

Letting go of the habit of self-blame and shame only happens when we can't stand the pain any longer. The moment when you look yourself in the eye and decide to let go is a moment you'll never forget. I always feel good when a student or client tells me how bad she feels when her inner voice is constantly blaming and shaming. She is miserable, suffering every day. Yet I have confidence because I know that the intensity of self-blame must increase to this very high level before change can happen.

I remember the moment in my own life. It was a peak experience of dramatic insight and relief, forever etched in my memory. After work one day I picked up my son from nursery school. I was driving up the hill toward home when I became aware of the constant and familiar stream of negative self-talk. Just as I rounded the last curve I realized that I couldn't stand it anymore. I couldn't tolerate the stream of criticism, blame and shame. I remember the scene in living color, the blue hood of the car and the high wall covered with ivy on the side of the narrow road. The refrain of self-scolding was going on all the time. In that moment I was scolding myself for not being home earlier so that I could prepare a nice dinner for the family. I felt pain in my gut and in my chest. I asked myself, why am I doing this? In that clear moment I made the commitment. I would let go of beating up on myself.

It was a big relief, but it wasn't a final victory. The habit was so ingrained that it returned again from time to time, giving me yet another chance to recognize it and let it go. Gradually it faded away; it became something that happened only occasionally.

In that precious moment I made a choice that profoundly changed my life. Because I was meditating every day I was ready to make the shift. Now I recognize my critical inner voice as a signal that something is bothering me. I need to spend a few moments alone with myself, checking in to my body sense about what I am feeling. At times I recognize a problem, something I need to change or take care of in my life. Once you make this commitment, just recognizing and acknowledging the source of the discomfort allows change and release.

The habit of negative judgment is extremely resistant to change. Now that you are bringing it fully to consciousness you will continue to work with it by reminding yourself to let go whenever you feel the familiar criticism, blame and shame. Letting go can provoke fear, because we rely upon this blame and shame as a central guiding principle in our lives. When you pass through the fear you will experience a deep sense of relief in your body.

Non-Judgmental Witnessing

Witnessing is simply watching your mind, your thoughts and feelings without judging, observing with a gentle and benign curiosity. The non-judgmental witnessing we are talking about here is a skill you have been developing since you began your practice. Witnessing, as we have learned, takes the place of judging and criticizing. It allows you to drop the judgment and finally drop old defenses. The defensive system you constructed during childhood was essential for your emotional and perhaps even physical survival. In advanced practice it will be obvious to you that the old system is an obstacle to your growth. The value of freedom to be yourself will be far greater than any need for the protection of your defenses.

Next time you find yourself judging and criticizing, notice how you feel in your body. Don't try to get rid of the sensation, but simply notice its quality. It is usually very uncomfortable, a sort of tightness or tension. Stay with it for a few moments. Follow the thread of the feeling back through time by asking when in the past you felt this same sensation. You may recall a particular time of painful blaming, criticizing and shaming you experienced as a child at the hands of your mother or father. Connecting with the body feeling evoked by a childhood memory is an opportunity to feel empathy and compassion for you, that little child who was left behind. Even if no new revelations come, you will recognize how long this has been going on. The blaming and shaming usually go back as far as we can remember.

To witness your own experience without distortion, even for a just few clear moments, is a healing opportunity. It allows you to see that you are simply a human being, once a child and now an adult, dealing with your life as best you can. This skill of neutral witnessing is the only way that you can get behind the firewall of your defenses long enough to see the full truth of what happened and where your defenses came from. Finally you can let go, let it be, and be at peace.

When you practice witnessing you can't help but see how you have tried so hard not to notice, not to feel the pain. In this healing process you will observe your defenses in action. They will come up in the moment when you get in touch with what you are feeling inside. Whisper gently to your deeper self and to the wounded child inside. Tell that small boy or girl it will be okay, it will be okay to feel all of it. You are stronger now; you can handle the feeling and even stay with it to allow it to change. This inner reassurance will help you to see why and how you've tried to protect yourself. Now it will seem natural to set these fear-based defenses aside so that you can see the truth, the whole truth of what happened.

Admitting the Truth

Despite all our efforts to shelter ourselves, many of us have conscious memories of traumatic events, accidents, illnesses, physical or sexual abuse, or of facing the dangers of neglect. Maybe you already know some of the basic facts of what happened. The memories you already have are the place to begin on your exploratory journey. As a wiser adult, you will rediscover the events with a far greater appreciation of their full impact.

You have a new start; you can face and make peace with the most painful and difficult issues of your past. Your progress will be much more rapid now that you have dropped negative judging, so that you are open to know, in the full light of consciousness, what you have always known deep inside. You will begin to see the whole course of your life with a clarity you never experienced before.

Trust your body to guide you toward healing and relief. The way to your truth is through attending to your body voice, the inner wisdom that is always available to you. When something important is coming to awareness you will feel the edge of tension in your body. It is a moment of anticipation. You are pregnant with the truth, and the discomfort can become so intense that you feel compelled to move through it. Stay with the feeling and trust the process. You recognize this extreme tension as a sign that relief is close at hand. This is the time to be fully honest. The whole truth not only embodies the facts of what happened but also includes the memory of the feeling, which you must allow fully into awareness. This bodily-based memory is the lasting residue of the event, the burden you have been carrying for so long.

Following the thread of the body memory is a more reliable and easier way to the truth than trying to remember it on a mental level. In order to penetrate to the truth and come to peace you need to feel all of it as it felt then, and notice your body sense of how you are carrying it even today. Usually the thread leads back to a time in childhood when you felt afraid, hurt and angry, even an episode of abuse that you did not previously remember or that you never before thought of as abuse. Now that you are willing to feel the whole of it, you recognize it for what it really was – and now is. You will come to trust and rely upon your body memory far more than you trust thought alone.

You will learn through experience that it is far less painful to move toward the truth and through it than to remain stuck. Moving toward the feeling, allowing the intensity to grow, is like passing through the eye of a needle. Your awareness will narrow to that one feeling-thread alone. Intensity builds and then, amazingly, it releases and fades. Release comes, and with it comes insight into exactly how it was for you, and how much it still hurts. Now the pain lifts, and it will never return. There will be many times when you will revisit old experiences with new eyes and will need to acknowledge more of the truth about what happened.

Here is an example of the deep healing we are talking about. Linda came to me for help with her meditation practice. She couldn't handle the feelings she was experiencing in daily sitting. She was depressed and she didn't know why. For her, seeking help was a matter of life and death; she was having suicidal thoughts and couldn't stand the pain. She had stopped work and gone home to live with her mother. She was terribly afraid of whatever it was inside that was making her so unhappy.

Together we discovered that Linda was a victim of childhood sexual abuse by her father. After a few months in therapy she began having flashbacks during meditation. At first they were only momentary fragments of images, but they carried tremendous fear. She saw her father coming in to her bedroom at night. When she told me about the images, she thought she must be fabricating them. How could they be real? She was so afraid of remembering and acknowledging what happened that she wanted to deny her own experience.

With my validation and support, she had the strength to get through the process of birthing the truth. She would come in to my office and lie down on the couch. At first it was simply to relax, but after a few meetings, I gave her some relaxation instructions and she spontaneously went into a deep state of trance. In the altered state she relived an episode as though it was happening right now. Week after week the sessions went the same way, she would say hello and talk for a bit and then lie down and go into trance almost automatically. The recollections came in her vision like movies, in vivid color and full of feeling. She remembered her father coming into her bedroom and raping her. The episodes continued for years.

Admitting the truth meant acknowledging the rape and the fact of her sexual arousal. She felt guilty because she was turned on, even though she was terrified at the same time. Linda was sure that the whole thing was her fault. She thought she had seduced her father, and it is true she flirted with him as all little girls flirt with their fathers. There was something about the sexual abuse that was enjoyable, but it was also an appalling violation and betrayal of trust.

The betrayal was doubled when she went to her mother, who refused to help her. Mother wouldn't do anything to stop the abuse. In that moment of recognition she lost both parents. No wonder she was suicidal. On top of all of this she felt guilty about confronting her mother. She knew her mother was too weak to leave her father.

The hardest part was the intensity of the fear she had to face, but she was able to go through it. Her body recognized the truth of the terrible betrayal and abandonment, and acknowledging the truth brought a wave of relief and relaxation. She was validating her own reality, letting go of pretending and denying. She experienced a time of deep sadness, disappointment and grief as she admitted the dreadful wound and all of its ramifications. The sadness and grief were part of her natural healing process.

After some weeks she reported that her sleep improved and her anxiety level sharply declined. She came to feel the rage that lay beneath her depression. As she continued to grieve, new memories emerged and she was ready to acknowledge them. Reviewing everything, she gained insight into what went on and how it had shaped her life. Her depression was lifting;

she was no longer feeling suicidal. She acknowledged how angry she was with her mother for not protecting her, and she recognized the awful irony of living with the mother she hated.

Linda's anger was powerfully validated by her body sense, the felt-certainty of her personal truth. In the moment she knew that the abuse was behind her fear and avoidance of men. It made sense that she was afraid of men and not attracted to them. She felt safe for the first time in her life. She felt the relief of knowing that the events of her childhood were in the past. She was now an adult and able to say no and protect herself, even from men. The terrible shame she felt about hating her mother was relieved in a blast of sudden awareness. She hated her mother because mother failed to protect her. This is heart-breakingly common for sexual abuse victims. If mother stands up for the child, she must leave the abuser. All too often mothers don't have the emotional strength, or the financial power to break up the family, so the child must accept the continuing abuse.

Finally she was able to put the responsibility for the abuse directly where it belonged, on her father and mother. She knew that she was innocent. She left her mother's home and started a new life, moving to a new town where she had friends and a job was waiting. She planned to continue her meditation practice after she completed her work with me and we said goodbye.

Linda's difficulty acknowledging the truth did not surprise me. She repeatedly denied the reality of the memories that kept coming back. She didn't want to believe herself. This is common among abuse survivors. It is painful to acknowledge sexual abuse. In fact, it is so painful and so frightening that it is easier to deny your own experience, what you see with your own eyes and feel in your own body, than to admit that your father or mother violated you this way.

For me it was amazing and wonderful to witness Linda's natural healing power at work. Her work taught me the power of the felt-certainty, the bodily-based recognition of the truth. Here you see a clear example of how connecting to this inner knowing gives us a solid base upon which to stand. It is a base that feels good inside; it fits with what we always knew. The felt-certainty is impossible to deny.

The Path of Healing

We each have our own unique and very personal history. But Linda's journey of healing is basically the same as the path we all must follow. Linda made a decision to trust and allow the memories. She had to face the fear that stood guard at the door. She had to remember the whole truth, all the painful details, including her mother's failure to protect her.

The path to relief is always forward, always moving toward the feeling, including even the fear itself. Often the first level of awareness is the emergence of unacceptable feelings you have pushed away in the past, such as hatred and fear of a parent. Whatever the truth, it is definitely worth knowing. The price of hiding is continuing a life of suffering, remaining stuck in the past, and that is no longer acceptable. Simply knowing the truth and how you felt and now feel about it is a blessing, no matter how ugly the truth may be.

You have the power. You have built the strength and the skills. You can and will feel the fear directly and be able to hold it in consciousness long enough to realize that it can't actually harm you. You are free, now that you have experienced its full strength and lived through it. After all, fear is only a feeling like all the others.

Now you are free and open to explore honestly the true meaning of all these events. You can even embrace the whole of the memory. This allows you to understand so many things about yourself and your life. The pieces of the puzzle fall together in a way that finally makes sense.

Now you see all of it from your point of view. You can side with you, instead of siding with the blaming, shaming parent. You remember what it felt like when it happened. You can see yourself as just a child, not really as bad as they thought. In fact, you were not bad at all, just being a child trying to get your needs met.

All our behavior is motivated by the primary drive for emotional and physical survival. Everything you've done and how you've lived your life in the past was a natural reaction to the conditions you had to cope with, a healthy effort on your part to deal with the circumstances of your life. When you can accept this positive point of view, you will see yourself from a more understanding and compassionate perspective.

Grieving

Now your heart can open to you, all that you are, the grown-up and the hurt child inside. You can acknowledge the longing and vulnerability, the pain and hurt, the anger, rage and hate. You can grieve for lost time, and for the changes you could have made, the lost opportunities to make better choices. This grieving reminds me of the many people who have said to me, with despair, "Oh how I wish I had started my meditation practice thirty years ago, or, I wish I had come to therapy when I first realized I was in trouble. My life could have been so much better." This recognition brings tears, but they are tears of compassion, tears of love and self-forgiveness.

Grief is a very important step in the healing process. It is inevitable, but it is not just another form of suffering. It is what comes when your heart opens to yourself. Grief comes from the recognition and deep acknowledgment of how much you have suffered, and it is part of letting go of the suffering so that you are free to move on. When you feel grief and sadness over opportunities lost or mistakes made, let it be exactly as it is. This is a healthy form of self-love, flowing from your heart.

Gently make friends with the new view of yourself as a vulnerable, lovable and loved human being and embrace it with caring loving presence. Comfort that small child and the grown-up soul within you who is so in need of your attention and love. Grief passes when it is accepted in the same way that you would accept any other feeling. From grief you will emerge into the light of clear and blameless awareness—this is what happened, this is how it was, this is how I felt and this is the way I feel now.

Transforming Self-Betrayal

We treat ourselves and others the way we were treated. If you had loving, supportive and valuing parents, you grew up instinctively understanding how to support and take care of yourself and your children. Conversely, if you were betrayed by your parents through abuse, neglect or abandonment, you grew up to betray and abandon yourself.

Self-betrayal and abandonment mean failure to provide for and protect yourself. You have trouble standing up for yourself, your rights and needs in relationships, at work and in life. This is the legacy of painful childhood experiences. If you were ignored or treated like an object rather than being honored and respected as a person, you will continue treating yourself in the same way, until healing interrupts the cycle.

We learn how to take care of ourselves by being consistently loved and cared for in childhood. Without this early patterning we are at a disadvantage. Since there is no such thing as perfect parenting, all of us have some deficits in our ability to love and care for ourselves. We need to fill those deficits and provide for ourselves what we needed from mom and dad.

Now we must learn a proactive way of self-care that is completely antithetical to punishment, betrayal and abandonment. It means learning to honor your feelings and put yourself first, placing your commitment to yourself before all others.

Imagine for a few moments that you had the perfect mother and father. What are the messages you so longed to hear, the words that would make everything all right?

The Good Mother Messages
Adapted from the work of Jack Rosenberg, Ph.D.

I love you
I love you just the way you are
You are special and important to me
It's who you are, not what you do, that I love
I will always be with you; I will even be there when you die
I want you
I see you and I hear you
You can trust me
My love will heal you and make you well
You can trust your inner voice; there are some things you
    just know
You can be different from me and I will still love you
Sometimes I say no and that's because I love you
You don't have to be afraid anymore

The Good Father Messages

I love you
I'm proud of you
I believe in you
I know you can do it
I will set limits and I will enforce them
If you fall down I will pick you up
You are beautiful and I give you permission to be a sexual
    being
I give you permission to be the same as I am, to be more
    than I am, and to be less than I am

The power of these simple words cannot be overestimated. When you whisper each message silently to the place in your body that is hurting, some of them will bring a strong response. Your body will let you know with a flood of feeling when you find the one or the several that you missed as a child. You might even recall a specific very early memory.

You may find that certain of these messages are central to your feeling of well-being. They are the ones that go to the most painful injuries of your early life. Many people have high abandonment anxiety. We are sensitive to any situation or event that triggers the feeling of being left alone. For us the words "I will always be there for you" are so important. Realistically, we know that we all die alone, even if our dearly loved partner is right there by our side. The truth is that you, the strong, grown-up, wise and loving you, is the one who will always and forever be there for and with you, no matter what.

I will never forget the first time I was presented with these messages and tried to repeat them to myself, from the mature strong me to the little girl inside who was left behind. I was hardly able to stutter out the very first one: I love you. I was taught that it was selfish of me to want to take care of myself and stand up for myself and my own needs. I have worked with these messages for years, using them to feel better when nothing else worked. There is always one that resonates in me, signaling what I long for right in this moment.

Some time ago David and I were talking about his life experience. When we came to the fourth message – It's who you are, not what you do, that I love – he recognized it as a clearly crystallized way of saying something that has always meant a lot to him. He needed this message as a child and through most of his adult life. He grew up feeling that he was loved for what he did rather than simply for who he is. Now he is free to be himself and love himself unconditionally.

You can actively practice the healing messages and give them to yourself, to your own small boy or girl who still lives inside you. Think of how you would give this loving message to your own child. With this work you are actually installing a new piece to fill in what you missed or to take the place of an old negative message that kept you stuck. You are repairing your operating system, and you are opening vast new possibilities. Now you have so much more room to breathe and to be yourself, unencumbered by the wounds of the distant past.

Taking Responsibility for Your Life

Taking responsibility is completely different from self-blame. It holds no punishment and comes through using clear vision to see our own character flaws and mistakes in judgment. Self-forgiveness means re-owning your deeds and misdeeds so that you can return with love to self-responsibility. First you must make amends for your own failure to be a good parent to yourself. Only then can you move on to taking responsibility for how you have treated others. How could you treat others any better than you have treated yourself?

New World Meditation rests upon the principle that we are all born innocent and pure and that there is no original sin. Whatever is bad or ugly, even hateful, vindictive or vengeful within us comes from the cumulative pain we carry, the scars of injuries that are still raw within us.

This applies to you personally. Now is the time to recognize, understand and accept the hurtful things you may have done in the past, whether to yourself or to others. You must bring to these difficult character issues the empathy, compassion and forgiveness that will allow them to heal, so that they no longer drive your decisions and push you into doing things that only increase your suffering.

What about mistakes in judgment, situations in which you did something you now regret? Perhaps you went along with a suggestion from a friend or family member, something you knew was wrong, or simply didn't fit with your true nature. Maybe you made a mistake in guiding your life that is now obvious to you. The first step in healing is admitting to yourself that you made a mistake.

In meditation you will reflect upon decisions you've made in the past that were based upon your old view of events, your old operating system, perhaps your own shame and self-blame. Now you can see and understand how these decisions worked against you. You can say simply to yourself: yes, this is what happened; yes, this is what I did. As you penetrate to the truth you are practicing your ability to remove negative judgment again and again.

You must ask inside more deeply about the cause of the error, the harm or the mistake. Where did this come from in me? You must continue looking within to discover the bottom line, the core, the crux of your action. And we come to the real question: "What was I feeling that led me to do this?" The process of self-enquiry is always the same; this is just another layer of self-exploration.

The feeling of inner peace you long for will come when you acknowledge the whole of it. The fact is that whatever you did came from your own feelings and your perception of your needs at the time. Mistakes and errors came from your own pain and injuries. They are not unforgivable sins. You will remember what happened and what it was in your life that hurt.

Maybe I did something that hurt someone I care for, and I feel bad about it. As I look back upon it I see it differently. I see that I was reacting to my own history and my own suffering. Now that I understand what I did and how it came from within me, I am open to acknowledging and asking for forgiveness. I feel no more anger and self-condemnation; instead I feel compassion for my loved one and I can disclose the feelings behind my behavior. This is truly making amends.

Repentance

In order to heal and forgive you must repent. You owe it to yourself. Admitting how poorly you have treated yourself is the first step in letting go of the old pattern. You must sincerely acknowledge your failure to care for and protect yourself. You must promise never to abandon or neglect yourself again and to be loyal and supportive to yourself. You can learn a new way of being present, a way of being with you when you need the essential companionship, friendship and attention that only comes with deep connection to yourself.

It is time to make a pledge to you. Here are the promises you must make to yourself to take full responsibility for your life:

The Pledge

I promise to love and cherish myself all through my life
I promise loyalty to myself
I will be loyal to myself even in intimate relationships, because my commitment to myself comes first
I promise to keep myself safe
I promise never to lie to myself, even for the purpose of protecting myself from a fearful truth
Knowing the truth is part of keeping my pledge to protect myself
I promise always to value and respect myself
I promise to take care of my health to the best of my ability
I accept my failings and past mistakes as part of my human condition

We often think that having a mate means we have to sacrifice our own needs in order to live up to our commitment to the other. Actually, relationships work only when each person takes responsibility for him or herself. I have a big responsibility. I am responsible for my own life and for taking care of myself, and it is a serious job. I know that if I don't take care of myself no one else will. No matter how much I love someone else, I know my first responsibility is to myself, to make the best and clearest choices I can.

The Way Forward

We cannot change what happened by wishing for a better past. We all want to jump ahead, and skip the part about acknowledging how much we were hurt. We want to let go of blaming others, especially our parents, because we feel guilty about holding them responsible for their deeds. What is forgiveness, this word we all use so lightly? Does it mean that I must honor my father and mother as a commandment? Does it mean that what was done to me as a child was OK after all? Does it mean that it never happened? I cannot say yes to this, because then I must return to self-blame. If my parent is not responsible then the responsibility must fall upon me, the child. Yet, holding the parent responsible means he or she is no longer the God/Goddess I wished they were. We are left with a feeling of loss, but it is the loss of a dream rather than of the reality.

We get to self-forgiveness through empathy for our own inner child, who was so hurt and betrayed. When we have empathy for ourselves we can see others with empathy, even those who have hurt us. With self-forgiveness I no longer suffer with hatred of my father, nor do I harbor thoughts of revenge. Now, I acknowledge the reality of what happened and admit that he is responsible. Now I see him in the light of empathy, as the flawed and imperfect being that he is. When you get to self-forgiveness, hatred of others who have hurt you simply falls away. Self-forgiveness is the end of suffering.

Twelve

Forgiveness

Now that we have worked through the most traumatic injuries, the most terrible events of our lives, we expect to feel free. In meditation we have clear moments of ecstatic bliss, but we still have those moments when we feel the pain of blaming and shaming. Even though it is softened by all our inner work, it still lurks in the background: a subtle sense of anxiety or sadness. It is the lingering shadow of the wordless self-blame, the default response, deeply embedded in the operating system.

What is this wordless self-blame, and why is it so hard to resolve this deep layer of suffering? In order to answer this question we must consider the most primary source of our pain, our very earliest experiences – the preverbal life of the infant. Most psychologists now believe that bonding with mother begins at the time of conception through the hormones transmitted in mother's blood, and continues all through childhood. This bonding is the most basic foundation of the operating system. Yet another look at early bonding will show you the sticking power of the residual pain we still face.

Forget for a moment that you are now grown up, and let yourself imagine what it was like for you, the new baby. You come into this world as a tiny helpless infant, completely dependent on mother. It is almost impossible for us as adults to imagine the profound nature of this dependency. For you the baby, mother is food, warmth and safety. Mother is life itself. Without mother you feel the pain and fear that come with hunger, which implies the ultimate threat of death.

Like most babies you are smart and intent, hungrily taking in all the available information from your environment, constantly processing everything around you in order to understand how the world works. It is essential for your very survival that you figure out how to get food reliably and be kept warm and safe.

Because you are helpless, you are vulnerable and must surrender, totally trusting in mother and father. You have no control over what is happening. You can only cry or smile and kick to communicate your needs. Whether those needs are met depends completely on mother. So you study mother's mood, her feelings, every action or expression.

But inevitably there are times when mother is not there for you. Sometimes mother is exhausted, she sleeps too deeply and has trouble waking up at your first cry. Sometimes there are problems in the family. Maybe mother gets sick and has to go away to the hospital for a few days. Yes, someone else takes care of the baby, but it is not the same as mother. You feel anxious and insecure.

These circumstances and so many others are unavoidable. Most of mother's mistakes and failures are natural and inevitable. No mother is perfect. Maybe you have colic or are cutting teeth. But that doesn't matter to you. You see mother as goddess, the primary source of all life. So when she can't make it better, you can only conclude that it must be your fault. There must be something wrong with you or she would fix it. The idea that it must be your fault, that you are somehow bad, is being installed in your operating system, right alongside the first principle that mother is life itself.

This is the deep root of our blaming and shaming, which is so hard to release. It happens so early in life that we have no words, no logical way of storing and recalling what happened. And so the wordless self-blame becomes the default response that is triggered automatically whenever we perceive abandonment or rejection. We carry this default response into adult life. We have no words for this pain, but the body remembers the feeling.

There are circumstances that can make the self-blame more intense. Because, as babies, we are psychically attuned to mother, we might sense that we aren't really wanted. Of course we assume that something must be wrong with us, otherwise mother would want us. When this occurs it makes the shame more pervasive. As adults we know that not wanting a child is mother's problem, not some fault in us. For baby, sensing mother's rejection leaves a lasting wound. This is just one example of what might go wrong. There are many other circumstances that might take mother's time and attention away from baby. Mother might have to go to work; she might have postpartum depression, or marital problems, to name just a few possibilities.

Then as you get a little older mother begins to scold when you spill your milk or make a mess with your toys. She might even spank when you scream with rage. Punishment is a powerful negative reinforcer. I am using the psychological term "reinforcer" to indicate anything mother might do that shapes behavior. In this case mother's displeasure or punishment heightens the power of the primary injury: her earlier unintended moments of neglect that you felt as abandonment or rejection.

Even with the best intentions, even when they truly love and want you, parents reinforce the seeds of insecurity, self-blame and shame. Like all of us you accept this naturally because it fits right in with your earliest feeling of inadequacy and rejection. We take it in and integrate it as part of our self-concept.

All of us carry this primary wound. It is the most basic source of the inner critic that is so hard to let go of. As we grow to maturity our true needs, beyond basic survival, are for love, acceptance and connection. We learn how to love by being loved; we learn empathy from receiving empathy. Some of us, the lucky ones, have this experience as children. Mother and father mirror love and acceptance and are able to attune to our needs and feelings. This kind of great parenting helps compensate for the preverbal self-blame but cannot overcome it completely. I was lucky. I was planned and wanted. Both my mother and father were delighted to have me. and I believe they loved me. However, mother told me later that she was proud that she had raised me by the book. She fed me every four hours, according to the prescribed schedule. She was told it wasn't right to pick me up before feeding time. If I was hungry early I had to lie in the crib and cry. Breast-feeding was not the fashion, so I was bottle-fed. Looking back on it from my adult perspective I realize how hard this was for me. I'm sure I felt cramps from hunger along with the fear that mommy would never come. This came home to me when my own baby boy cried with hunger every two or three hours. It was grueling for me to keep up with his needs, but I fed him whenever he wanted it. I know from other mothers that most newborns need to be fed quite often, and I feel sad when I think of the millions of babies who were fed "by the book."

I grew up with a lot of criticism. I could never be quite good enough. I remember lying awake in bed at night wishing that I could somehow be a better girl so that mommy would approve of me. Maybe you have memories like mine. Maybe you worked at being a good boy or girl, doing what was asked of you, even though you hated it. Or maybe you were angry and rebelled, raging openly at the punitive or abusive parent. No matter which way you responded, the underlying injury is the same. The wordless self-blame becomes a basic truth that we rely upon as we try to make sense of all the events of life.

As we grow older we replace the external scolding parent with our own inner judge. Most of us grow up thinking that driving ourselves to be perfect is the only way we will succeed in life. The negative self-talk comes back as a remnant of that primitive hunger-driven fear of abandonment and death. The automatic default response of self-blame is always there.

Even as adults we continue trying to find ways of making ourselves better so that we might win mother's love. Of course we don't think that this is about mother at all; we don't recognize the early roots of this dynamic. We learn to scold ourselves as mommy or daddy once did, in the hope that we can be good enough to be accepted by society, the other kids at school, the friends we make at college, the boss and our fellow workers, our wives and husbands. The wordless self-blame is rooted so deeply in our reality that it remains untouched. No matter how successful we are in life, it is never enough.

Self-blame works for us. It keeps us in line with society's expectations and usually leads to the rewards that act as replacements for the love we truly desire. And so we are enslaved to the substitutes: money, status and power. Our dedication to these substitutes comes to dominate our lives. But inside we are still in pain. The replacements, the pseudo-rewards, never fill the real longing, for love and acceptance. The substitutes are never enough, but we know nothing else, and so we drive ourselves for more, always clinging to this hopeless quest.

You can't ever remember the actual moments, the events that planted the seeds of shame within you. But your body remembers the feelings that surrounds those moments just as if it were happening today. We have only the body feeling, the ill-defined unease inside, tightness, pain, even illness and disease.

It is only through working with the bodily-carried wound that you can finally connect to the self-blame that hides inside. When we connect directly with this feeling it doesn't seem to melt and diminish with the loving attention we give. It keeps coming back, continuing to haunt us. In advanced practice, your body will bring to light the actual sensation and emotion that surrounds the core injury. In clear moments you will be strong enough to feel the feeling and be curious, welcome it and be open to exploring it. You will notice that as you sustain attention on the feeling you can connect directly with the body sensation, the tension and discomfort that always accompanies shame and self-blame. They always feel bad. After a time you know exactly what is happening; you will instantly recognize the distinctive sensation-based signature of self-blame. But you can't really work it through, as you have so many other feelings. Because of its preverbal roots it won't release as other feelings have. And because of your months and years of practice your body voice is alive in you, always letting you know how much it hurts and demanding that you pay attention.

The Spiritual Crisis

As you stay with your practice there will come another unforgettable moment. Every day as you sat in meditation you come face-to-face with this painful and subtle but pervasive feeling of insufficiency, inadequacy, self-blame and shame. Finally you can no longer avoid your imperfection. From this point on there is no way back.

This is the bottom line. You are facing the same impenetrable wall faced by all the monks in all the monasteries day after day for all the years that they spend trying to come to Enlightenment. Now you must come to the crucial leap of faith. Am I going to trust my body to guide me to a new reality? Or am I going to continue to cling to the old paradigm, the self-blame and shame that I have based my life upon? And the pain is so great that amazingly, in one clear moment, you know that you're ready.

Finally you decide to trust yourself. What else can you do? You can no longer go on as you have. And, to your amazement, you find it is not such a big leap after all.

Eckhart Tolle, best known as the author of *The Power of Now* and *A New Earth*, describes coming to self-forgiveness as instantaneous, but his release was presaged by almost thirty years of suffering. He wanted to kill himself when he was six years old because he felt that he was so intrinsically bad. Over the years he was always miserable. His inner self-talk continued, brutal and abusive. He was filled with self-hate. When he was twenty-nine he arrived at a turning point. He couldn't stand beating up on himself anymore, and he had to give it up. This was his moment of Awakening. He realized that he was hearing the internalized voice of the critical parent, constantly blaming and shaming. He knew he had to let go. He had the thought that he couldn't live with himself any longer. He made a choice to accept himself just as he was.

In this moment everything in his life was immediately transformed. Even his visual perception was enhanced. Everything looked brighter and more colorful. He was so surprised that he didn't know what to do with himself. What happened here for Eckhart was that he realized that this foundational piece of his operating system could be changed. In fact, in this crisis it did change. It released. He was left in the ecstatic bliss of no more shame and blame. But he was left without a compass, without his old operating system. He had nothing to replace it.

The path of NWM is different from Tolle's experience. The Body/Mind Wisdom will replace the old piece of the operating system, the blame and shame. To find out what's missing for you, what went wrong way back then, we must ask the body. Through experience you already know that your body recognizes the truth when you say it, and it signals that recognition with a definite response that we call the felt-certainty. You can easily and directly connect with your Body/Mind Wisdom by reciting those good parent messages to yourself, out loud, while looking in a mirror. You will find it is harder than you imagined. For me, as I wrote in Chapter 11, it was the very first that was the hardest—I love you. I'm sure there is one that fits for you too, one that resonates strongly inside, in your gut or in your chest. Your body's response points directly to your injury. Now you see it for what it is.

You have prepared for this change through repeated experiences of moving through bodily-carried pain to relief and release. You are making an intentional leap to a new level of trust in your own Body/Mind Wisdom.

We can't ever change what happened in the past or fix our imperfect parents. But recognizing the root of the injury, the source of our vulnerability, eases the pain and helps us to see that we are not alone after all. The grown-up, strong part of us can give us the love we so needed as a child.

Surrender

Surrender is yielding to true humility. It is giving up your old reality of self-blame and shame, as well as the defenses you set up to protect you. You are giving up the illusion of invincibility and perfection, the defense you have used for so long. Self-forgiveness and acceptance are the only way forward.

Surrender will come as a profound relief. It comes not in admitting that you are bad, inadequate or flawed. Relief is in acknowledging that you are human, with all that implies. You need love and acceptance, and we all have needs we can't meet by ourselves. Our very existence depends on getting food and having warmth and safety. We need intimate connection, touching, being held: feeling loved by another and by ourselves. We need the intimacy of sharing feelings with other people. This is not a weakness or a flaw. It is simply the truth of our needs which cannot be filled by any material thing, wealth or power.

Any choice other than acceptance of our full human condition will lead only to more suffering. Reality is on our side; none of us is perfect nor ever will be. Mother was imperfect too. She failed us in myriad ways that she couldn't even know. She was only human, just as we are. We can't possibly heal the self-blame without accepting her imperfections as we do our own, exactly as they are.

And finally you come to the shocking truth: you are fine just the way you are!

You are amazed to discover that there is no pain in admitting your flaws, weaknesses and wounds. Your fears of surrender were only imagined. Just like all the other truths you have confessed, this is something you have always known. It is just that you spent so much time and energy hiding it from yourself and everyone else. Now you can drop all that and just be who you are.

You are just a regular person doing the best you can. You cannot be anything other than what you are. Maybe you are dark-skinned rather than fair; you may have straight hair rather than curly; perhaps you are short rather than tall; if you were born poor, you were not born rich. Even though you may think of these as your flaws and weaknesses, they are actually just the circumstances of life, for which you cannot be blamed. Self-blame feels bad inside. It is the signature of suffering. It carries unease, tightness, pain, illness and disease. We are clear on that now.

All the flaws of parenting that fueled the wordless self-blame are the inevitable result of the karma you brought into this life, the multigenerational injuries, the wrong choices and the slings and arrows of outrageous fortune carried by your ancestors. The family you were born into was flawed, as we all are. Now you see your struggle to survive and thrive in this family as part of your journey to this moment of acceptance. You can see your parents and siblings and their suffering as clearly as you see your own.

Resetting the Default Response

The new default response is a core bodily-carried sense of security, based on self-love and self-acceptance. This is the felt-certainty of inner truth. This confidence and security is much stronger than any you have imagined in the past, because it is based upon the Body/Mind Wisdom, always with you. This will be your new compass on the path of life and will define your new reality.

You see things differently now. This wisdom, the decision to feel good rather than bad, is your new default response; this is the Body/Mind Wisdom you have learned to connect with. Your body is now the place where you go to check in, to see what feels right. You will naturally default to self-care and self-respect. You will replace the imperfect love and care of your mother and father with your own limitless self-love and forgiveness.

Self-forgiveness and the healing it brings means doing what makes you feel better rather than mistreating yourself.

As an example, what if you get fired from your job? In the old paradigm getting fired would instantly trigger the wordless self-blame and shame. You would feel loss, hurt and rejection, and hear the parental voice saying you are bad, worthless and no good. You cave in to the suffering and withdraw for days or weeks. Finally you are able to go look for another job, but you feel weakened inside, so you are less confident, which acts as a handicap in your search.

Now your response is very different. You have resilience. You acknowledge the reality of being fired, and you immediately notice the feeling in your body. You spend some time exploring your reaction. Although there may be regret, and a sense of rejection, there is no feeling of shame. It has been replaced by curiosity. In meditation you reflect upon the job and what happened, and explore your responsibility in the situation, and the role of others, as well as outside factors that may have influenced the firing. You own the part that was your responsibility and allow yourself to learn from it.

Through this process of exploration you come to a feeling of resolution. You know how you participated in the dysfunction that led to the firing. You recognize that the job wasn't going well and that you were uncomfortable. It wasn't a good fit for you. You have gained insight that will help you to find a right next step. You feel good as you explore new opportunities that await you. You may be surprised to find that you feel better, even relieved.

Forgiveness

This is the spiritual transformation: finally reaching self-forgiveness and letting go of the preverbal shame. Forgiveness allows you to give up the old way in favor of the Body/Mind Wisdom, far more reliable as a guide along the path of life. Following the Body/Mind Wisdom feels good, and so it is positively reinforcing. Here I am using the term "positively reinforcing" to point out that feeling good makes you want to continue feeling good. Every time you choose a path that feels good, it strengthens your sense of security and your confidence in your choices.

Healing is the gift of self-forgiveness. In the instant that we surrender to self-forgiveness our view of the past is completely changed. Now we can see clearly all of whatever happened, and see it in a new light. We have finally reached the longed-for healing we spoke about at the beginning of this book.

You have made the leap. You know that you are fine just the way you are. This is all there is to it; this is forgiveness!

PART FOUR:
COMING TO AWAKENING

Thirteen

The Existential Dilemma

We have come to the last bend in the trail and ahead, looming out of the mist, we see the final peak. There is yet one more challenge that we must overcome. It is the inescapable existential dilemma of impermanence: the ultimate certainty of death.

The Buddha believed that it is impossible for us to accept impermanence. We live with the abiding fear of illness, disease and death. Our lives are dominated by this pervasive fear and all the things we are compelled to do in our vain attempt to ward it off. As a consequence of this limitation, all of life is suffering. In the Buddhist view the cycle of death and rebirth is the most painful reality we face. He referred to this as the endless wheel of Samsara. Suffering is only ended by reaching Enlightenment.

The Truth of Impermanence

Impermanence is logically obvious and undeniable. Every day we see the constancy of change all around us. Like all life, like every flower, we are born, we blossom, reproduce, fade and finally die. Our lives are always vulnerable in the constant fire of destruction and creation. Ultimately each of us has to face their own death.

David and I accept the Buddhist idea that denying impermanence of all things and the consequent inevitability of death can only lead to fear and suffering. So why is death, this obvious reality, so difficult to accept? One might think that our fear of death has to do with the mystery of what happens afterward. But there is a much more serious obstacle to acceptance, and this obstacle is impossible to overcome.

Our ability to accept impermanence is limited by the structure of the brain itself. Until recently it was thought that all fear is based in the amygdala in the midbrain. Recent research suggests that there is a deeper root to the survival imperative, beyond the need to reproduce. (Feinstein et. al., 2013) Survival is hard-wired into the brain at the most primitive level: in the brain stem. This primary instinct is not available to conscious thought, so the drive to avoid death is not something we can talk ourselves out of. This is one reason why actually letting go and dying seems to be such a long and arduous process. Many people who are terminally ill and in pain openly state their readiness and willingness to die. They want to go, and yet the physical vehicle hangs on, prolonging their suffering.

In addition to the hard-wiring of the brain, we have our conditioned learning. We have learned to experience fear surrounding everything that is even remotely associated with death, anything that implies the possibility of injury to the body. These fears are a survival mechanism. They work to keep us out of dangerous situations. They are stored in the midbrain, the emotional part of the brain. Here they live on. And they rule. Our avoidance of danger is deeply ingrained, almost completely unavailable to conscious control.

And so we have an internal conflict. On the conscious level, the logical level, impermanence makes perfect sense. On the emotional level accepting impermanence is supremely difficult. On the instinctual level it is impossible.

Let us explain what we believe is possible. What happens if we attempt to accept impermanence on the emotional level, where we have some capacity? Consider its implications, its meaning for us as human beings, and how we might cope with the inevitability of death in the light of our practice of NWM.

Death is the ultimate mystery. Not only must we face the prospect of death itself, but we must also contend with the terrible uncertainty of the when and how. Several years ago a young woman came to me for help; I will call her Mary. She was suffering from acute traumatic shock with severe anxiety. She told me that just a few days ago she was driving down a major boulevard in the city. Coming toward her she saw a blue sedan. Suddenly the sedan veered across the double line and hit her car head-on. Fortunately she had a new SUV, well-equipped with airbags. She sustained some injuries but nothing significant. What really frightened her was the dead body she saw on the pavement in front of her. The woman driving the oncoming car had a heart attack, became unconscious and drove across the line. Right there on the pavement Mary saw how quickly and unexpectedly death can come. She was young. She came from a background of insecure parenting; she felt vulnerable as a result. It had never occurred to her that death can come at any time. The accident reminded her of her early life, when she felt alone and on her own in a dangerous world.

She continued to see me to ground herself in the security of our relationship, which she knew she could rely upon. In our conversations, which went on over several months, we talked about the reality of impermanence. We talked about her wisdom in buying the new car that protected her with advanced safety features. All of us have to live with the reality of impermanence and uncertainty through every day of our lives. It is simply a fact. If you are lucky enough to survive into old age you will become acutely aware of this reality and of the preciousness of each day. Mary's task was to come to terms with the human condition.

We all carry the fear of illness and disease and of the pain and suffering that accompany them, as well as fear of the deterioration of the body, loss of function and all the eventualities that precede death. We have a terrible fear of helplessness and dependency, which symbolize the prelude to death and recapitulate the helplessness of infancy.

At the same time, any discussion of death is taboo. Any reminder of death, no matter how remote, is to be avoided. It is hard for us to talk about death even when we are facing it directly. Too many families of the critically ill fail to tell them the truth about their prognosis. We say we want to protect the dying loved one, and that may be true but not the only truth. We are also afraid of the intense feelings of the dying person, and the possibility that he or she might openly speak of it.

This is a sad betrayal because it denies the woman who is sick a chance to think clearly about her death and what it means to her. It denies her an opportunity to review her life and say goodbye to loved ones. The denial of death robs us of the richness of this critical part of the human experience. Although we rationalize that we are doing it to protect her from the reality of death, we do this for selfish reasons, in order to protect ourselves from the truth of our own looming loss, our grief and our own inevitable death. The taboo about death robs the dying person of her sacred opportunity for conscious dying. It is a betrayal of our responsibility to each other.

Attachment

Attachments and desire dominate our lives. We are driven to accumulate things and develop behavior patterns designed to feed the illusion of permanence. Remember that the insecurity of infancy feeds the need for attachment, first to mother's love and then to the objects that serve as substitutes. Collecting material things and money gives us the illusion of security, and so things we collect and things we do in the service of denying death multiply endlessly. We have to have more and more because nothing can really ward off the fear of death, so we can never have enough. Excessive attachments drain our energies and resources, offering only superficial comfort. It is not the things themselves that are the problem. It is all the energy we put into them, the grasping, the clinging and the distortion of our perceptions that surround them that are the source of suffering. Suffering is inevitable because of impermanence. Everything we have we will finally have to give up.

The Egyptians built gigantic pyramids in which they entombed the dead king, including even his servants, who were killed as part of the funeral rite. They took all manner of material goods with them, on the assumption that they would need them in the afterlife. Now we recognize the absurdity of trying to take it with you. Yet we spend a great deal of money on funerals, caskets, burial plots and fancy trappings. All of these are attempts to comfort us for the loss of loved ones and shelter us from the reality of death. Our funeral rituals, while not as elaborate as the Egyptians, still offer us the illusion of permanence. We buy the heavier, more costly metal casket imagining it will somehow protect our loved one from complete decomposition. We pay for embalming for the same reason, even though we know it won't preserve the body for long.

Some material things are necessary and appropriate. For instance I believe the Dalai Lama has attachment to his glasses, which he wears all the time. Yet he is not consumed by his attachment. He has no need to wear fancy glasses, or to have 40 pairs. If he lost them I'm sure he would peacefully adapt and get a new pair.

We are all subject to the allure of excessive attachments through illusion and glamour. Illusion is distortion on the mental plane. Sometimes things, such as a big stone mansion with a fine slate roof, appear to be so strong that they are immune to loss, giving us the illusion of permanence. In reality the house will probably last longer than we do, but eventually even a stone castle will crumble into ruin.

Glamour is distortion on the emotional plane. Under the influence of glamour things are imbued with emotional loading, giving them a glow of attraction. A clear example is the aura of attraction imparted to images in advertising. Advertising executives know that the television car ad is the highest paying work they can get. They compete viciously for car company business. Car ads are super-glamorized. A recent one showed the mouth and lips of a woman glowing with red lipstick even before you saw the car. Then you see the big black car speeding through the night, with the beautiful scarlet-lipped woman in the passenger seat and the older good-looking man at the wheel. The man (presumably the potential buyer, rather than the woman, who is viewed as an object, the passive recipient) is given the message that he is in charge, powerful and attractive to women. Women are given the message that men with fancy cars are worthy of their attention and especially attractive as mates. An acquaintance of mine told me she first decided to date her husband when she saw him behind the wheel of his black-on-black Corvette. In that moment she knew that this man would be her husband.

The Marlboro man was a fictionalized character designed to glamorize the destructive habit of cigarette smoking. The ads showed him looking healthy, handsome and perpetually immune from death. He was the strong, silent type, riding off into the sunset. In fact the actor ultimately died of lung cancer. In this case the glamour not only distorted our perception of smoking but concealed the harm.

Money is highly glamorized. We behave as though we believe having a lot of money means we will be happy, better than other people, secure and somehow immune from death. It is true that people who have enough money to buy healthcare live longer, but buying healthcare does not require millions or billions.

Glamour affects even the most basic attachment, which is to the body itself. We try to protect the body with medicine and proper food, and this is appropriate. But the deification of doctors is glamour; the compulsive acquisition of expensive medicines even when they are not necessary or won't give us the cure we desire is glamour. Doctors may symbolically represent the possibility of permanence, but they cannot prevent death, even though they may delay it. They are subject to the same mortality as the rest of us. We spend millions every year on cosmetic surgery, not to mention all that we spend on fancy creams designed to deny and disguise aging. We feel compelled to look as young and attractive as possible, in order to deny even to ourselves that we are aging, and will ultimately die.

Glamour is insidious and pervasive. Much of the time we are unaware of the distortion it causes. We do need a roof over our heads and enough healthy food to eat. But we exaggerate and magnify our needs, until a roof becomes a mansion and healthy food becomes filet mignon. The richer we are the more money we spend on acquiring things in our endless quest for shelter from impermanence. But the reality is always there. In fact, steak is not good for us; it contributes to an earlier death. Mansions can become a burden; they require a great deal of maintenance, ongoing expense and attention. You always have to worry that someone will break in and steal your valuable possessions. You are vulnerable to fire, earthquakes and financial reversals.

Under the influence of glamour our attachment to material things grows out of control. Greed is endless. Things are endless; there is always another thing, nicer and more elaborate than the one we have. One car is never enough; ten is far better. Ultimately we can be consumed by the glamour of material things.

These attachments to material things serve the dream of permanence, even though all material things eventually deteriorate, decompose, dissolve or end up in a landfill, and eventually return to the earth. From ashes to ashes, dust to dust.

The Buddha was right when he saw that hanging on to attachments is a cause of suffering. It is futile, painful and wrought with fear. It is a burden that acts as a handicap to the joyful experience of the now. He believed that the only relief from suffering comes from the release of all desire and all attachment. He saw no other way out of this final dilemma. With the release of all attachments you have nothing to lose, and hence you have no fear of loss and no suffering. Material attachments offer superficial excitement and pride in possession. But in reality they are only a temporary shelter. They fail to satisfy; they are only entertainment for the ego.

Except for the attachment to the body and to the personal self, all other attachments are optional. We choose our attachments, the amount of time and energy we put into them, and how we manifest them.

David and I advocate wise discernment. Carefully choose for yourself what you truly need and want, and consider the price in time, energy and responsibility. When you think carefully about the difference between need and want it is not so hard to choose. Beyond basic needs, we find love and human connection to be the most satisfying things in life.

Yes, we need material things, and we can enjoy them, but it is the attachment, the clinging itself, the illusion of permanence, which is a lie and creates suffering. Glamour, illusion and the attachments they support melt away once we face the reality of death, along with the fear that will naturally accompany it. Death is a normal part of life and an inescapable part of being human.

Fear of Death

Fear is just a feeling, and like other feelings it passes through the body in a wave. Even the most daunting feelings, fear and grief, build to a peak and then recede like the tide. The fear of death is so primitive and so powerful that it will always be the ultimate test. The survival imperative will always be with us. Ultimately we will all have to face it. We know we can't make this fear disappear, but we also know that we can survive the direct encounter. It is not the fear that will kill us. So at least on the mental and emotional level death is not as threatening for us as it once was.

In daily practice over years we cannot avoid facing fear at one time or another. The fear of death is no different; it is intense and inescapable. It cannot be healed and laid to rest like other fears. But you do have experience in dealing with fear of things you cannot change. It is this experience that will prepare you for the fear of death, to whatever extent it is possible to be prepared.

Sogyal Rinpoche, one of our favorite Buddhist masters, said the purpose of meditation is to prepare for death. As a Buddhist he believes in reincarnation. He sees the process of dying as an opportunity for raising consciousness, to maximize your progress as you transition to a new life. (Rinpoche, S. 1993)

You don't have to believe in reincarnation to benefit from your meditation practice as preparation for death. Your experience in healing will allow you to die with strength and dignity. As you approach death you will feel the fire of fear. But since you expect it, you can look forward as you see the approach of death, face it, acknowledge it and let it be just as it is. You will feel the fear, and since there is no way out, you will look it in the eye.

You can never resolve the fear of death, but you can put it aside for a time by recognizing and acknowledging it each time it returns. Yes, there you are again, my old friend, I know you, I recognize your power, now can you sit down here next to me and wait for a while? Approaching death will never be wonderful, but it will be better than it would otherwise be, because you are prepared. You can be truthful with loved ones and say the things that need to be said. You will look over your life and lovingly say goodbye to your family.

Yielding

Change is so constant and pervasive that denying impermanence is as desperate and hopeless as trying to cling to a mossy rock in a fast-flowing river. Hanging on is painful. The river of change bombards us with more force than we can possibly overcome. All the things we do to avoid the fear of death are sources of stress to the human organism. Inevitably we will be exhausted, which only invites illness and disease.

Impermanence is the flow of perpetual change within which we live our lives. We choose to yield to that flow rather than fighting and continuing to suffer. Change is the constant unfolding of the now. Each moment is born from the one before. We never know what comes next, and the possibilities are endless. This is one of the wonders of life. Like the journey up the mountain, there is always another bend just ahead and we can't see around it until we get there. Something wonderful is always possible. Joy is the reward.

Fourteen

Awakening

We come to Awakening over years of practice, gradually replacing old values and fear-driven behavior patterns with new ways that feel far more congruent with our true selves. We make decisions based on our genuine needs and wants rather than the distortions caused by illusion and glamour. We have reached a state of comfort that comes with healing, acceptance and self-forgiveness. This foundation enables us to live more easily, with far less anxiety and with love to spare for those around us who are suffering. This congruence gives us a deep and abiding sense of satisfaction with life.

The New Consciousness

Daily practice gradually brings the body-knowing and the mind-knowing together to form the Body/Mind Wisdom. Your body voice is seamlessly merged with your mind voice. This flow carries much more information than either body or mind alone can encompass. It is no longer an experience you have only during meditation. Coming to Awakening means that you stream this expanded consciousness all the time. Each action, anything that happens, from the smallest incidental encounter to the most momentous and important event, is felt and thought about in every moment of unfolding awareness.

Awakening changes your experience of reality, and the change is permanent. You can never go back, nor would you want to. You cannot turn off your body voice when you think it is inconvenient; it is a powerful force guiding you toward what is good for you. You will no longer put up with being mistreated or try to ignore mistreatment in order to do what you think is expected. Nor do you mistreat yourself as you have in the past. You will automatically honor the Body/Mind Wisdom because you have learned through experience that ignoring it or overriding it will lead you off the track of your deepest intentions into false choices and mistakes in judgment.

Your new life is based upon a radical principle: now you guide your life in a direction that feels good, a life that is uniquely suited to your true essence. Feeling good is not just a mental construct. It is a body-based sense of well-being. The Body/Mind Wisdom is the realization of the fully developed Self, your home base, the compass that guides your life. It happens one day at a time, one moment of choice at a time. Moments of choosing what feels good blend into days and years that feel good. It is not difficult to decide because the Body/Mind Wisdom is always there. This is the felt-certainty of personal truth and you are living it every day.

Values

In the old reality we were always struggling to cope with two major issues. First, we were trying to make up for lack of self-acceptance and interpersonal connection with money and power. We were caught up in the endless accumulation of things. Now we have that essential self-love we have always longed for. We value human connection far more than excessive material things, and because of our increased confidence we are capable of relationship. We seek out meaningful activities and cultivate relationships that meet our real needs.

Second, we were compelled to deny the truth of impermanence and the inevitability of death. We tried to ward off this fear by the accumulation of excessive and unneeded possessions. We used illusion and glamour to feed and support our denial of death. We were enslaved by false attachments, squandering our energies in the never-ending quest to ward off the fear.

In Awakening we surrender. We accept the truth of impermanence. We accept death as a normal part of life. We always knew it was real; we just tried to ignore it, cover it up and pretend it wasn't there. Denying this reality drained energy and fed anxiety. Now we admit we will feel fear as we approach death, and we accept it as a part of life. It comes as a relief to acknowledge this truth. The acceptance helps us to appreciate each moment, each day, and the preciousness of every living thing.

Morality

When we were children we learned a sort of morality based on fear. We were afraid of the shame and pain of getting caught and punished. Some of us learned that God would rebuke us and we would go to hell if we behaved in a way that was "bad." On the other hand if we were good boys and girls and did the "right thing" we would go to heaven after death. Growing up we learned what was legal and what was illegal and that we could be caught, shamed and punished for violating the law. So our choices were always motivated by fear.

Now our morality is based on empathy, the capacity to feel what it is like to be the other person. There is a more advanced principle, "Do unto others as you would have them do unto you." This principle has been around for thousands of years. It is a clear statement of the truth of empathy. It means that other people are the same as we are; they have needs and feelings that we must consider in framing our actions.

From the very start of your practice you have cultivated the capacity to be empathic. With the Body/Mind Wisdom, empathy is more than a thought or just a word, it is a body experience. Something is different inside. Empathy is always living and breathing in your body, so that when you hurt someone you feel their pain. When you treat others well you feel the comfort you bring them. Our morals and values are no longer imposed by any outside authority or fear of punishment. Now they come from within.

Now it is clear why honesty is so important. In the old way, we told lies out of shame. We were trying to cover up parts of ourselves or feelings we thought were unacceptable. Lies are always based on the assumption that we are not acceptable the way we are. Telling lies feeds this negative and undermines our self-esteem, making us feel worse about ourselves.

In your new world, you know deep inside that you are fine just the way you are. You no longer need to hide your true self, and thus there is no longer any need to lie. Telling lies feels bad and so you avoid it. Since you are comfortable with yourself it is fine, in fact it feels good to let others know the truth about how you feel. Even small "white lies" are no longer necessary. When you are dishonest you will feel discomfort because you rob yourself and others of the truth.

You know the truth when you hear it, and you know untruth when you hear that. In your body, in your gut, there is a sense of relaxation and rightness when you hear the truth. When you hear lies you will empathically feel the anxiety and even fear in the body of the liar. Your inner voice speaks, whispering mistrust.

Our morality is simple and easy to understand. We now have an internal compass, guided by the Body/Mind Wisdom, our new default response. Empathy is always with you. It is a natural result of your openness and enhanced sensitivity. Your own personal suffering is over, yet you see and feel the pain and suffering of others around you. Your heart opens to them.

Compassion

It is reported that the Buddha said, "Compassion is that which makes the heart of the good move at the pain of others. It crushes and destroys the pain of others; thus it is called compassion. It is called compassion because it shelters and embraces the distressed."

Here the Buddha is saying that it is compassion itself that is healing. When you are Awake you too can and will bring comfort by your very presence. It can be as simple as sitting with another person, listening and reflecting their feelings in a way that allows them to heal. You convey compassion by being fully present and giving loving empathic attention. Your inner reward system has been changed. Comforting others brings joy to your life and you want more.

Yes there is and always will be hunger and desperate poverty. You cannot possibly end all the suffering endured all over the world. You, like all of us, are limited by your own personal resources. When you see people in front of you who are hungry you will give what you can. But if you exhaust yourself you will be unable to help anyone, so you must pace yourself and conserve your own health. Choose carefully when and how to give most effectively. Remember that compassion itself carries tremendous healing energy. It empowers and inspires people in their struggle to meet their needs and the needs of their families.

You identify with those who are suffering because you too have suffered. Your heart is open. You feel unconditional love and understanding radiating directly from your heart to the sufferers all around you. It is the unconditional accepting love embracing all that it is to be human.

With healing you are fused into the wholeness of your being. No part of yourself is rejected, ignored or abandoned out of shame. You accept all of who you are. With this wholeness you can be compassionate. You have plenty, you are secure in the abundant flow of self-acceptance and self-love, and so it is natural for you to be loving, giving and sharing.

The blessing of self-forgiveness makes it possible for you to forgive others as you forgive yourself. With self-forgiveness your suffering is ended. As a consequence of healing you are no longer consumed by hatred of those who have hurt you in the past. This anger and hatred was part of your burden of suffering. Now you see even those who have harmed you in the light of compassion. They too are only human and beset by their own pain, which they may not have the strength to face. With new eyes you see and accept yourself and others as perfect in our imperfection, limitless in our limitation and whole in spite of our injuries.

Empathic compassion brings humility. Our shared reality is inescapable, for us and everyone around us. Each of us is on his or her unique path, each struggling to learn and grow through the lessons of life. We are all humble as the plain naked human beings we are. This is the wisdom of real humility.

Like you, David and I see the struggle of our fellow human beings around us, and we respect it, but we realize that we cannot remove all the pain, nor can we end all the suffering. All of us must deal with the struggle for food and shelter, and the dreaded reality of impermanence. We are blessed to have refuge in our daily practice.

Authenticity

Awakening will allow you to express your true nature. For the first time in your life you can live as the person you truly are, complete with all your flaws as well as your beauty and your strength. You recognize that you do have needs and desires and weaknesses, but now you no longer have to cover them up. You can be open and transparent because you no longer feel compelled to defend yourself from your own disapproval, or the rejection you used to expect from others.

Now you are free to be and to live exactly as you are. You no longer spend time and energy trying to figure out how to conceal things about yourself that you are ashamed of. You are not afraid to be honest with yourself about what you see and hear, your personal truth, your feelings, thoughts and opinions. Being fully authentic eliminates a major source of stress, benefiting your health and maximizing your creative potential.

Intimacy

We always longed for intimacy, but we assumed that the love we experienced was all that was possible. There was always the longing that could never be satisfied. At the same time, because of our shame we were terrified of being fully seen by another. We feared that if anyone saw us as we truly are, we would be rejected. We were trapped in our defensiveness, always needing to cover up our flaws and imperfections yet caught in the longing for love. This was a major cause of our suffering, but how could we know what we were missing? We just knew a constant subtle feeling of deprivation, loneliness and isolation.

Living authentically means that your potential for intimacy and love is now fully available. You are open and unafraid. It is natural and comfortable to be known as who you are. In fact, it is what you have always longed for. Now you can feel the sensation, the joy of love flowing abundantly through your heart to the dear ones in your life. Moments of true human contact are precious peak experiences. You like yourself, and so you naturally assume that others will like and even love you.

Friendships are more rewarding. You are no longer self-conscious, preoccupied with being acceptable, and so you can be fully interested in your friends. You want to understand their feelings and what it feels like to be them. You are fascinated by the different experiences and perspectives of others. You can disclose your feelings openly, which invites others to be open, so all your relationships are more nourishing for your friends and for you.

Now that you are healed and you know that you are fine just the way you are, you have a much greater chance of having a lasting and loving relationship. You are no longer hung up on pride, trying to prove you are without fault. You can work things out with your partner, admit when you are wrong without shame and stand up for yourself without guilt.

In sexual intimacy you will be more completely turned on in your body, because you are no longer afraid that your excitement will be seen by your partner. Free of fear orgasm becomes a full body experience. You will have times of true intimacy, listening and disclosing to your partner in a way that leaves you feeling well-fed and deeply satisfied. This intimate connection will bring you improved health and increased longevity, as well as an ongoing sense of joy and happiness.

In the past, love always carried the risk of loss. Now, for us, love is worth the risk. We're not afraid to love because we know we have strength and resilience. We have healed from prior losses, and we know we can survive and grow, even from lost love. Loving is a risk we want to take because the rewards are so great.

Creativity

Dropping pretense means your energy resources are fully available for the blossoming of your natural creativity. You have no fear of fully expressing yourself. You no longer fear the judgment of others. Creative process fills a need almost as powerful as our hunger for food, it is inherently satisfying. You can take a chance and try something new. It might work: it could be beautiful, it could be useful and it could be emotionally moving. Your essence will bloom and expand to fulfill your potential. Through expressing your unique self you create original work.

Our creative process is another channel for sharing joy in human connection. Self-expression is our gift: ideas, thoughts and feelings we experience and then convey to the world. We share our unique experience of life. It turns out that other people can relate and find meaning in what we thought was ours alone. When others understand our message we feel the joy of connection.

Creativity lives in many forms. It can come in traditional ways, such as art, music or writing, but it also comes in approaching any problem and solving it, no matter what form it takes. Creativity is figuring out how to fix the car, make a delicious meal or touch another person in a pleasurable way.

Being creative always involves taking a chance, trusting your own impulses and your sense of what you're trying to convey. When you give your creativity full reign you are empowered to make a living in a way that is satisfying in the deepest sense.

Work as Spiritual Service

Now work is inherently fulfilling, and you live in the profound satisfaction of your spiritual service. Not all of us spend our time building houses for needy people or serving food in shelters. Even though you may go to the same office or shop every morning, you appreciate the ways in which you are serving humanity. If you repair cars you are helping people get where they need to go, to home, work or school. If you run a factory you are providing jobs to people who can support their families with the wages you pay. You pay a living wage, because to do otherwise would feel bad to you. There is nothing wrong with making money through your service. But making money is not the only reason you work. You work for the joy of your calling. Being productive and helping others feels good.

Even if you have a menial laboring job, your work is still your spiritual service. Maybe you build roads by digging with a shovel, bending your back over and over all day. You are making it possible for people to travel from place to place more easily. Most importantly, through your work you provide food and shelter for yourself and your family. Women who work at home also do their spiritual service: birthing nurturing and bringing up children, the most important contribution to society. All work contributes to the betterment of humanity in some way.

Living in the Now

With Awakening we feel the exquisite pleasure of being fully present, the essence of mindfulness. In the moment-to-moment flow of life every activity takes on extra color and aliveness. With all the months and years of practice we chipped away the old painful reality. Finally it is gone, to be replaced with our new life, joyful and filled with confidence.

Before healing we were always threatened with a repetition of past trauma or other events like them. We projected these injuries out ahead of us, poisoning our vision of the future. This looming threat actually led us to repeat the mistakes of the past and re-create the pain. Fear of the future kept us from being in the present in the current moment. This was part of our suffering, which is now ended.

Daily happenings can still be upsetting, but with the Body/Mind Wisdom fully engaged, most issues are processed within a few minutes. Significant losses cause pain and take longer to work through, but we no longer hang on to pain. Coming to self-forgiveness we are complete with our personal past, so that we can let it be and leave it behind. Inner conflict is resolved and so we are free. Free of preoccupation with the past and the future, we are fully present in the joy of the now.

The Buddha said that all of life is suffering. But most of our suffering is ended. We accept impermanence. We yield to the flow of change. We no longer deny the reality of illness, disease and death and the inevitable fear we know we will experience. We can accept this because we know how to meet fear with self-compassion. Because we have resilience and strength we can die with dignity.

Now that we are fully mindful we see the beauty of each living being. In the light of impermanence, every living thing is a beautiful miracle. We honor all forms of life, plant and animal, as truly amazing and wonderful. We love the beauty and perfection of even the insects. It is a miracle that a butterfly, so beautiful and delicate, so vulnerable, can even survive.

You know you can handle any eventuality. You are comfortable living in the flow of constant change; in fact you love it for its excitement and aliveness. You meet the future with joy and hope instead of dread. With healing you see magic in the possibility that always lives in uncertainty. The future is constantly unfolding here and now, every moment holding the promise of new experience.

Yielding to impermanence brings us to living in the now. Any other choice leads only to further suffering. Now that you are whole, you allow yourself to embrace and fully experience whatever comes in life. This is living life to the fullest, in the energy and excitement of the now.

Awakening and Enlightenment

What we call Awakening is not Enlightenment in the Buddhist sense. Enlightenment, the ability to live with compassion/wisdom, is yet another advanced state. It implies that we sustain compassion all the time, a continuous flow of limitless unconditional love, always available. It is true that we often experience compassion/wisdom, but we cannot sustain it in every minute of our lives. We are and always will be growing and evolving, a work in progress.

David and I think of empathic compassion as the one consciousness that can someday unite us all. Even though much of humanity cannot yet be with us in this new way, we already have many companions who are on the path. What we have discovered is not our own unique knowledge. We think of this potential as the truth that lives deep within each and every human being, even though only some are aware. With empathy and compassion we share the human condition, with all that it implies: our struggle to accept impermanence, our limitations, suffering, strength and resilience, joy and happiness.

Awakening is returning to love, the love which has always been our ultimate potential. With the heart opening of self-forgiveness, love and compassion flood from your heart, flowing freely all through your body. You feel compassion for yourself, for your loved ones and for all other sentient beings. You are a channel for the limitless flow of universal love.

This is the ecstasy of Awakening!

Bibliography

Bowlby, J. (1973). *Separation: anxiety and anger.* New York: Basic Books.

Bowlby, J. (1988). *A secure base: parent-child attachment and healthy human development.* New York: Basic Books.

Bowlby, J. (1997). *Attachment.* London: Pimlico.

Brach, T. (2003). *Radical acceptance: embracing your life with the heart of a Buddha.* New York: Bantam Books.

Brazelton, T. B., & Cramer, B. G. (2012). *The earliest relationship: parents, infants and the drama of early attachment.* London: Karnac Books.

Brefczynski-Lewis, J. A., Lutz, A., Schaefer, H. S., Levinson, D. B., & Davidson, R. J. (2007). Neural correlates of attentional expertise in long-term meditation practitioners. *Proceedings of the National Academy of Sciences, 104*(27), 11483–11488.

Brown, K. W., & Ryan, R. M. (2003). The benefits of being present: mindfulness and its role in psychological well-being. *Journal of Personality and Social Psychology, 84*(4), 822–848.

Buddhavacana. (2014, February 11). In *Wikipedia, the free encyclopedia.* Retrieved from http://en.wikipedia.org/w/index.php?title=Buddhavacana&oldid=583034496

Chödrön, P. (2001). *The wisdom of no escape: and the path of loving-kindness*. Boston; [New York]: London : Shambhala ; Distributed in the United States by Random House.

Cozolino, L. J. (2006). *The neuroscience of human relationships: attachment and the developing social brain*. New York: Norton.

Damasio, A. R. (2000). *The feeling of what happens: body and emotion in the making of consciousness*. New York: Harcourt Inc.

Davidson, R. J. (2000). Affective style, psychopathology, and resilience: brain mechanisms and plasticity. *The American Psychologist, 55*(11), 1196–1214.

Davidson, R. J., Kabat-Zinn, J., Schumacher, J., Rosenkranz, M., Muller, D., Santorelli, S. F., Sheridan, J. F. (2003). Alterations in brain and immune function produced by mindfulness meditation. *Psychosomatic Medicine, 65*(4), 564–570.

Dayananda Saraswati: The profound journey of compassion | Video on TED.com. (n.d.). Retrieved from http://www.ted.com/talks/swami_dayananda_saraswati.html

Epstein, M. (2013). *Thoughts without a thinker: psychotherapy from a Buddhist perspective*. New York: Basic Books.

Feinstein, J. S., Buzza, C., Hurlemann, R., Follmer, R. L., Dahdaleh, N. S., Coryell, W. H., Wemmie, J. A. (2013). Fear and panic in humans with bilateral amygdala damage. *Nature Neuroscience, 16*(3), 270–272.

Gendlin, E. T. (1981). *Focusing*. New York: Bantam Books.

Gendlin, E. T. (1998). *Focusing-oriented psychotherapy: a manual of the experimental method*. New York: Guilford Press.

Goleman, D. (2005). *Emotional intelligence*. New York: Bantam Books.

Goleman, D., & Goleman, D. (1988). *The meditative mind: the varieties of meditative experience*. New York: G.P. Putnam's Sons.

Gray, L. (1977, August). *A study of pregnancy, body image and anxiety*. Unpublished Doctoral Dissertation.

Gray, L. (2013). *Focusing - learn from the masters* (2 edition.). Los Angeles: New Buddha Books.

Grof, S., & Halifax, J. (1978). *The human encounter with death.* New York: E.P. Dutton.

Heller, L., & Lapierre, A. P. (2012). *Healing developmental trauma: how early trauma affects self-regulation, self-image, and the capacity for relationship* (1 edition.). Berkeley: North Atlantic Books.

Holmes, T. H., & Rahe, R. H. (1967). The social readjustment rating scale. *Journal of Psychosomatic Research, 11*(2), 213–218.

James, W. (1950). *The principles of psychology Vol. 1.* New York: Dover-Publ.

Kabat-Zinn, J. (2005). *Wherever you go, there you are: mindfulness meditation in everyday life.* New York: Hyperion.

Kabat-Zinn, J. (2013). *Full catastrophe living: using the wisdom of your body and mind to face stress, pain, and illness.* Published in the United States by Bantam Books.

Kübler-Ross, E. (1997). *On death and dying.* New York: Macmillan.

Kübler-Ross, E. (2011). *To live until we say good bye.* Scribner.

Lazar, S. W., Kerr, C. E., Wasserman, R. H., Gray, J. R., Greve, D. N., Treadway, M. T., Fischl, B. (2005). Meditation experience is associated with increased cortical thickness. *Neuroreport, 16*(17), 1893–1897.

Levine, S. (1982). *Who dies?* New York: Doubleday.

Lewis, T., Amini, F., & Lannon, R. (2001). *A general theory of love.* New York: Vintage Books.

McCall, R. B., & Carriger, M. S. (1993). A meta-analysis of infant habituation and recognition memory performance as predictors of later IQ. *Child Development, 64*(1), 57–79.

Miller, A. (1983). *For your own good: hidden cruelty in child-rearing and the roots of violence.* New York: Farrar, Straus, Giroux.

Miller, A. (1996). *Prisoners of childhood: the drama of the gifted child and the search for the true self*. New York: Basic Books.

Miller, A. (2006). *The body never lies: the lingering effects of hurtful parenting*. New York: W. W. Norton.

Nhất Hạnh, Ho, M., & Vo, D. M. (1987). *The miracle of mindfulness: an introduction to the practice of meditation*. Boston: Beacon Press.

Nhất Hạnh, & Kotler, A. (1991). *Peace is every step: the path of mindfulness in everyday life*. New York: Bantam Books.

Ogden, P., Minton, K., & Pain, C. (2006). *Trauma and the body: a sensorimotor approach to psychotherapy*. New York: W.W. Norton.

Partanen, E., Kujala, T., Näätänen, R., Liitola, A., Sambeth, A., & Huotilainen, M. (2013). Learning-induced neural plasticity of speech processing before birth. *Proceedings of the National Academy of Sciences, 110*(37), 15145–15150.

Perry, B. D., Pollard, R. A., Blakley, T. L., Baker, W. L., & Vigilante, D. (1995). Childhood trauma, the neurobiology of adaptation, and "use-dependent" development of the brain: how "states" become "traits." *Infant Mental Health Journal, 16*(4), 271–291.

Piburn, S. (1993). *The Dalai Lama, a policy of kindness: an anthology of writings by and about the Dalai Lama*. Ithaca, N.Y.: Snow Lion Publications.

Rinpoche, S., Gaffney, P., & Harvey, A. (1993). *The Tibetan book of living and dying*. New York, N.Y.: HarperCollins Publishers.

Rosenberg, J. L., Rand, M. L., & Asay. (1985). *Body, self, and soul: sustaining integration*. Atlanta, Ga.: Humanics Ltd.

Siegel, B. S. (1990). *Peace, love & healing: bodymind communication and the path to self-healing : an exploration*. New York: Perennial Library.

Siegel, D. J. (2001). Toward an interpersonal neurobiology of the developing mind: Attachment relationships, "mindsight," and neural integration. *Infant Mental Health Jornal, 22*(1-2), 67–94.

Siegel, D. J. (2007). *The mindful brain: reflection and attunement in the cultivation of well-being.* New York: W.W. Norton.

Siegel, D. J. (2012). *The developing mind: how relationships and the brain interact to shape who we are.* New York: Guilford Press.

Stern, D. N. (2000). *The interpersonal world of the infant: a view from psychoanalysis and developmental psychology.* New York: Basic Books.

Stern, D. N. (2004). *The first relationship: infant and mother, with a new introduction.* Harvard University Press.

Stern, D. N. (2004b). *The present moment in psychotherapy and everyday life.* New York: W.W. Norton.

Stern, D. N. (2012). *The interpersonal world of the infant: a view from psychoanalysis and developmental psychology.* London: Karnac Books.

Suzuki, S., & Dixon, T. (2010). *Zen mind, beginner's mind.* Boston: Shambhala.

Teicher, M. H. (2002). Scars that won't heal: the neurobiology of child abuse. *Scientific American, 286*(3), 68–75.

Trungpa, C., Baker, J., & Casper, M. (2002). *Cutting through spiritual materialism.* Boston; [New York]: Shambhala ; Distributed in the U.S. by Random House.

Trungpa, C., & Gimian, C. R. (2010). *Shambhala: the sacred path of the warrior (Shambhala Classics)* (Reprint edition.). Shambhala Publications.

Weiss, L. G., Saklofske, D. H., Prifitera, A., & Holdnack, J. A. (2006). *WISC-IV advanced clinical interpretation.* Academic Press.

Acknowledgments

We were honored to work with Norman and Roberta Owen, who edited and critiqued the book as we went along. Norman is a lifelong friend of mine, a professor of history, author and editor of several books. His wife Roberta worked with him on this project and has become a dear friend. They companioned us both emotionally and intellectually for many months, always patient and supportive, even when I balked at the task. Their work with us was truly a gift of love.

I deeply appreciate the thoughtful support and criticism of my writers group here in Costa Rica: Greg Bascom, Lenny Karpman, Carole Marujo, Hobbit Merritt, Michael Crump, Chris Clarke and the late Jo Stuart, much missed. The group gave me a hard time in a number of meetings, but always with hugs, and I thank them for being themselves and feeding me good lunches while we argued.

I have received great support from the Focusing Institute, especially fellow Coordinators who are friends and colleagues of many years. I thank my teachers, especially Gene Gendlin, Linda Olsen Weber, Robert Gerard, Ed McMahon and Pete Campbell, who gave me roots in Focusing and meditation.

We are grateful for the love and support of our family and friends who have missed us at so many parties. We have received great encouragement from Irma and Marty Hawkins-Kasindorf, and Dorrie and David MacArthur, our best friends back in Los Angeles.

Finally we want to express our deep gratitude to Costa Rica, this beautiful, peaceful country. Being here gave us the beauty, the quiet (except for the birds who are always singing) and the time we needed to birth this book. It is where we find peace of mind, the precious support for our practice. We can float in the ecstasy of bliss as long as we like.

About the Authors

Lucinda Gray is a psychologist in international practice. She is the author of *Focusing, Learn From the Masters*, available at amazon.com

David Truslow is her husband and partnered with Lucinda in creating this book. Together they are teaching New World Meditation, and offering support groups to people all over the world who want to build and sustain a regular meditation practice. They work via the web, in individual sessions, and in workshops.

They live in Costa Rica, the only country in the New World to have abolished the army, and adopted peace as a way of life. They live high on a mountain in the central valley, where the orchids bloom and the birds sing every day of the year.

They can be contacted at:
www.NewWorldMeditation.com
In Costa Rica at 011 (506) 2228-2041
USA at 001 (310) 827-4241

Made in the USA
Lexington, KY
03 April 2015